Guide to Accountability in Music Instruction

Guide to Accountability in Music Instruction

Joseph A. Labuta

Parker Publishing Company, Inc.
West Nyack, New York

Library of Congress Cataloging in Publication Data

Labuta, Joseph A
    Guide to accountability in music instruction.

    Includes bibliographical references.
    "Selected source guides for instructional media": p.
    1. School music--Instruction and study--United
States. I. Title.
MT3.U5L2   780'.72   73-9973
ISBN 0-13-367953-5

To Karen, Joe and Steve

how this book will help you

The concept of accountability is affecting all educational programs in today's schools. Parents, politicians, administrators and lay people want to know exactly what is being accomplished in each classroom. They want proof of the value of each course.

This book contains a basic plan of action that music teachers can follow in accepting the challenge of accountability, and provides guidelines and workshop material for an in-service training program through which directors of music and supervisors can work with their whole staff toward accountability. It is a simplified, practical guide that leads you step by step through the procedures used by performance contractors who offer money-back guarantees that they will be successful.

Components of accountable instruction include: a systems approach, behavioral objectives, assessment, criterion-referenced measurement, instructional media, teaching/learning strategies, systematic instruction, and entry and exit tests. Perhaps these terms seem technical, theoretical and unrelated to music teaching. However, I think most people discover, some time in their formal or informal education, that nine-tenths of the difficulty in learning anything new is becoming acquainted with the jargon. To restate this in a positive way, the terminology of a discipline or area of knowledge consists of concise statements of the underlying ideas or con-

7

cepts that structure it. We will come to grips with the jargon and relate the important ideas to music teaching.

This book will equip you to fulfill accountability standards by applying the systems approach to your teaching. You should be able to write behavioral objectives for your courses and construct appropriate measures to determine your students' present capabilities and assess their skills at the end of instruction. You will also have a sound basis for choosing teaching procedures and instructional media.

Appendix A gives actual examples of musical objectives and instructional systems, to help you prepare your own objectives and a system for reaching them. Sources of educational media are provided in Appendix B.

If music is not to become peripheral to public education, we must develop accountable programs that will receive adequate resources and support. We must define the objectives of our music courses and prove that they are being achieved by the majority of our students. The procedures and techniques described in this book will help music educators in their efforts to put a program of accountability into action.

Joseph A. Labuta

acknowledgments

Although it would be impossible to name all of the people who have contributed in some way to the writing of this book, there are several who merit special thanks and recognition.

Many public school music teachers and university professors provided ideas, materials and comments. They include Elizabeth Hays White, Robert Sidnell, Ray Roth, James Harris and the individuals listed separately in Appendix A.

Professors Tom Burford and Tom Roberts of Wayne State University contributed their knowledge as specialists in instructional technology, as well as their reference materials. Professor Al Stahl, also of Wayne State, spent considerable time reading the manuscript. His reactions and recommendations were most helpful.

Douglass Campbell must be singled out as the devil's advocate whose creative approaches to curriculum development influenced much of the thinking contained in this volume.

table of contents

11

Guide to Accountability in Music Instruction

1

building accountability
into your music program

There is little doubt that we have entered into a new era in public education. The powerful notion of accountability has affected many school programs, and its influence is being felt increasingly in school music. The demand for accountability has grown with the rising costs of public education and the concurrent dissatisfaction of students, parents, politicians and lay people with the results of this education.

Accountability has quite literally turned things around in the schools by placing emphasis upon what students learn, not upon how they are taught. In addition to emphasizing ends over means, accountability entails: 1) improvement of instruction through systematic decision-making; 2) clearly defined learning outcomes, agreed upon prior to instruction; 3) independent assessment or audit by qualified outside personnel; and 4) public report of the results of assessment. This chapter provides a simplified, practical guide to help music teachers understand accountability and the related systems approach to education.

What Accountability Can Mean to Music Teachers

Some school music teachers with whom I have talked resent the idea that their successful music programs and their proven teaching methods should be criticized and perhaps condemned as a result of some new educational fad. They feel threatened and react in a negative, hostile way. Others are apathetic: they feel that too much fuss is being made over something with which they have lived for a long time. Good teachers have been accountable forever. They have always had a good idea in the back of their minds about the things that students ought to accomplish (implicit objectives). They have always worked hard, using appropriate methods and materials, to help students succeed. Finally, they have always "known" whether or not students have succeeded and have felt responsible if students failed.

Furthermore, music teachers, as a group, have always been held accountable as few other teachers in the school have. Their musical organizations must perform in public and be evaluated many times each year. Concerts, half-time shows, programs and festival ratings provide ample proof of results.

Although no one can deny that musical performance is essential to the music program, group performance alone is no longer accepted as a measure of musical accountability. Accountability means that music teachers are responsible for the learning of each individual pupil as well as for the training of bands, orchestras and choruses.

Accountability is not a negative concept. A positive application opens up many possibilities at all levels of the music program. Accountability, with its related systems approach to education, should help good teachers do an even better job. The systems approach provides a solid basis for decision-making and action. Using objective data, you can decide to continue, terminate or change existing programs. It is a new way of thinking. It presents a challenge and a certain excitement. It can mean these things to you and your teaching:

1. You are in control of the teaching/learning situation.
2. You develop performance objectives for student learning.
3. You develop procedures, try them, and revise them on the basis of assessment results.
4. You cause learning. You have evidence of results.
5. You no longer go through a method book lesson by lesson. It takes you out of the "method book rut."
6. Students move at their own pace. Talented students are not held back by others.
7. You do not have to teach the way you were taught. Rather, you teach the objective to which you are committed.
8. The systems approach provides an alternative answer to the lock-step traditional teaching structure and the seemingly unstructured open classroom.
9. It can change the way you look at students to a positive and optimistic outlook. You are causing your students to learn.
10. You are concerned with each child. Mastery learning requires individual achievement. A student is recycled if he does not reach objectives in his initial attempt.

Good music teaching has always been concerned with musical objectives and with effective methods, materials and evaluation—hence with accountability. The systems approach makes these more explicit. It is a commitment to improve teaching and student learning. You decide what students should be able to do after instruction, "teach" them, and then prove that they can, in fact, do it.

Input/Output

In the accountability approach emphasis is placed on student learning outcomes, not on teacher performance, methodology or administrative practices. In other words, the educational program is judged primarily on its *output* rather than its *input*. (See Figure 1-1.) This is quite a shift from the usual accrediting procedures. Accrediting agencies have been evaluating school systems using such

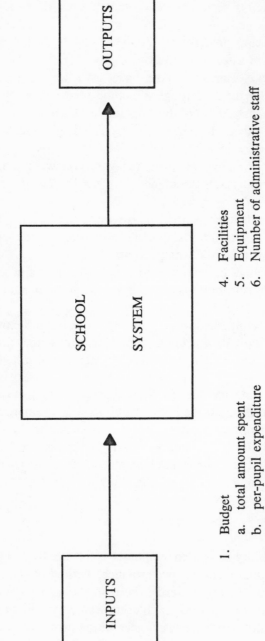

INPUT VS. OUTPUT IN ACCOUNTABILITY

INPUTS

SCHOOL SYSTEM

OUTPUTS

1. Budget
   a. total amount spent
   b. per-pupil expenditure
2. Number of teachers
   a. student/teacher ratio
   b. class size
3. Qualifications of teachers
   a. number with certificates
   b. number with master's degrees

4. Facilities
5. Equipment
6. Number of administrative staff

Results of the educational program—
Learning outcomes as demonstrated
by individual student performance

Figure 1-1

criteria as teacher-pupil ratio, per-pupil expenditures, number of teachers with certificates and master's degrees, number of books in the library, types of courses offered, and other indices of teaching methods, administrative procedures, equipment, and facilities. These are all examples of input measurement.

The emphasis now is on output. The focus is on the end product and the proof of performance. The measurement cannot be in broad, general terms open to many interpretations. It must be in precise, unequivocal terms. Thus a clear statement of performance objectives is a number-one prerequisite.

Extent of Teacher Liability

Accountability is a legal, ethical and moral obligation in every profession. However, a teacher should not be held accountable unless he knows at the outset the educational results for which he is responsible. Again, the results of teaching, the outcomes, must be clearly specified in terms of student behavior. These outcomes should be agreed upon in advance by all people involved in the educational endeavor. It becomes obvious that instructional-level objectives cannot just be handed down from on high. Teachers must have a part in the development of objectives and have a deep commitment to them. Most teachers will not teach toward objectives to which they are not committed, just as most students will not work toward objectives to which they are not committed.

Furthermore, the accountability model is designed for management control. If teachers are to be held accountable they must also have some decision-making power over the resources needed to reach the objectives. They must have the schedule, equipment, materials, facilities and budget to effect the desired outcomes. This problem has been approached by some teachers through an "in-house" performance contract. In essence it states that the teacher will produce specified results in an agreed-upon amount of time, given needed resources.

Teacher responsibility, in the final analysis, must be judged by the standards of "good practice" in music teaching. Albert Shanker of the American Federation of Teachers has warned that a teacher cannot be held accountable for results that depend upon factors not within the control of the teacher or the school. Therefore, he argues that

> Competent practice is *not* necessarily related to some particular performance result. It would be unwise to evaluate a doctor, for example, on the basis of the number of patients who die while in his care. If the doctor concerned is a cancer specialist, the difficulty is obvious. Here the question of competent practice may have more to do with whether he prolonged life, or relieved pain.
> So what is missing in our field of education, and must be developed in conjunction with the accountability movement, is a model of what a competent practitioner does when faced with a particular set of problems.[1]

We can agree that unrealistic outcomes should not be imposed upon a teacher and that outcomes should reflect the actual teaching situation. Yet the systems approach to education, which emphasizes both the *process* and the *product*, offers a viable method to achieve accountability. (We might still wonder about the competence of a doctor who lost too many patients or a lawyer who lost too many cases.)

The Systems Approach to Education

To be realistic and workable, accountability must be based upon a systematic approach to instruction. The idea of systems in the sense advocated here may need some clarification. In the following pages the notion of systems approach and systematic instruction is developed for utilization in the accountability model.

Systems in Music

Systems are nothing new to music. Systems of one type or another have been utilized for years in many areas of music educa-

---

[1] Albert Shanker, "Accountability: Possible Effects on Instructional Programs," in *Accountability in Education,* Leon M. Lessinger and Ralph W. Tyler, eds. (Worthington, Ohio: Charles A. Jones Publishing Company, 1971), p. 71.

tion. For example, most university marching bands have their own well developed systems for getting the job done effectively and efficiently during the hectic fall football season. At another level, elementary instrumental music programs are required to fill the needs of junior and senior high school performing organizations. Many authorities advocate and most successful instrumental programs utilize elaborate "feeder systems" designed to achieve this goal.

Method books and graded elementary music series books also purport to provide orderly, systematic approaches to school music instruction. A system, in this sense, is a planned approach to a goal, utilizing available resources to the best advantage. It is systematic, but it is not *the* systems approach. Notice also that the previously mentioned systems are group oriented. They emphasize group results, not individual learning. Thus none is acceptable as such for accountability.

The Cybernetic Cycle

The systems approach used for accountability has its roots in common sense and the nature of man's functioning intellect—the cybernetic cycle. Cybernetics in human action refers to control by the mind and central nervous system. Perceptual input through the senses (sight, hearing, etc.) is stored and processed in the brain. Here, on the basis of this information, decisions are made to reach a goal. Then an actual attempt is made to reach the goal. Subsequent action is based upon the success or failure of the attempt. Modification or reinforcement occurs as a result of feedback or knowledge of results. Feedback provides either confirmation of correctness or data necessary for change, modification and improvement. (See Figure 1-2.)

At the common sense level, this cycle helps us improve as music teachers. We try new methods, materials and techniques to achieve our teaching goals and evaluate their effectiveness. The common sense way can be outlined something like this:

1. We get an idea about how to solve a teaching problem. It may be an original idea, but more than likely it is ac-

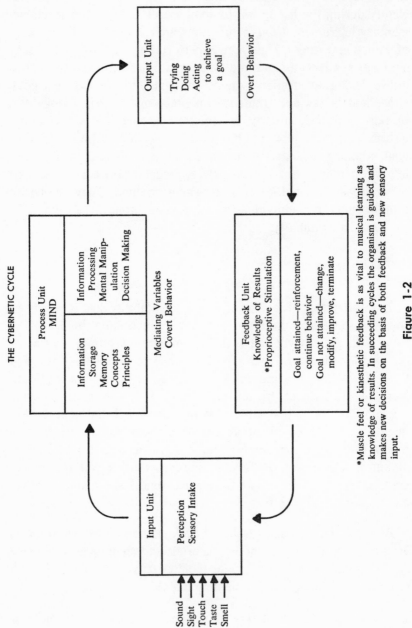

THE CYBERNETIC CYCLE

Output Unit

Trying
Doing
Acting
to achieve
a goal

Overt Behavior

Process Unit
MIND

Information
Storage
Memory
Concepts
Principles

Information
Processing
Mental Manip-
ulation
Decision Making

Mediating Variables
Covert Behavior

Feedback Unit

Knowledge of Results
*Proprioceptive Stimulation

Goal attained—reinforcement,
continue behavior
Goal not attained—change,
modify, improve, terminate

Input Unit

Perception
Sensory Intake

Sound
Sight
Touch
Taste
Smell

*Muscle feel or kinesthetic feedback is as vital to musical learning as knowledge of results. In succeeding cycles the organism is guided and makes new decisions on the basis of both feedback and new sensory input.

Figure 1-2

quired from a colleague, workshop, clinic, book or journal.
2. We try it.
3. We see how it works.
4. We keep it if it is successful, and modify it or drop it if it is not.

The process is rather casual. The evaluation is based upon an informal interpretation of results or student reaction to the innovation. It is an example of the cybernetic cycle operating in the day-to-day functioning of a music teacher.

Cybernetics has come to mean much more than this crude illustration however. It is the science of control of information, communication and/or action based upon the model of human intelligence. The cybernetic principle has been applied to all manner of man-made entities in the form of artificial intelligence. Its feedback and self-modifying aspects are most important. The home heating system is often used as an illustration. (See Figure 1-3.) The cooling system of an automobile is another example. Both are self-correcting or self-adjusting systems controlled by a detector and regulator —the thermostat.

Systematic Instruction

The systems approach developed from the cybernetic cycle or, at least, from the application of artificial intelligence to computers and machine technology. It is a method for decision-making with subsequent action and necessary modification for improvement. According to Banathy, the systems approach is "common sense by design. A self-correcting and logical methodology of decision making to be used for the design and development of man-made entities."[2] It is a way of thinking and doing that provides a viable procedure for improving the teaching/learning process.

A "system" has been defined as an organization of parts interacting as a unit to achieve a purpose. More technically, it is a structure (a synthesis of all interrelationships) made up of interact-

---

[2] Bela H. Banathy, *Instructional Systems* (Palo Alto, Calif.: Fearon Publishers, 1968) p. 91.

ing and interdependent parts (components or elements) that do something (function) in some way (process) to achieve the goal (purpose, objective or product). There is also an assessment component (detector and evaluator) that monitors the extent to which the purpose has been achieved by the system and a feedback loop for modification and improvement.

A flow chart is generally used to describe the system. It freezes the components and yet indicates the functions, processes and interrelationships. Like any organically functioning unit, a system is more than the sum of its parts. It is not a mechanical, cause-and-effect chain of events. This notion has been at the root of the criticism that the systems approach to education is dehumanizing. More will be said about this in the next section.

Figure 1-4 shows a simplified instructional system. It is a subsystem within the total school system[3] and is comprised of the following components: 1) behavioral objectives to indicate what each student should be able to do at the end of instruction, 2) preassessment to ascertain what the student needs to learn, 3) instructional strategies and media to facilitate learning what is not known, and 4) a posttest to assess student progress and teaching effectiveness. The system recycles and modifies on the basis of feedback. A complete course developed from this model is accountable when the implications of each step are considered, and when outside assessment is included with ongoing teacher-pupil evaluation.

Is the Systems Approach Inhumane?

Music, as a fine art, has long been justified as a humanizing force in education. Critics maintain that the systems approach is

---

[3] Whereas this book limits the use of systems to the practicing music teacher, the reader is urged to study the following references that develop the systems approach for the administrator, curriculum designer, and instructional technologist.

Banathy, *Instructional Systems*.

Jack Crawford, ed., *CORD, National Research Training Manual*, 2nd ed. (Monmouth, Oregon: Teaching Research Division, Oregon State System of Higher Education).

Dale G. Hamreus, "The Systems Approach to Instructional Development," in *The Contribution of Behavioral Science to Instructional Technology* (Monmouth, Oregon: Teaching Research Division, Oregon State System of Higher Education).

John McManama, *Systems Analysis for Effective School Administration* (West Nyack, N.Y.: Parker Publishing Company, Inc., 1971).

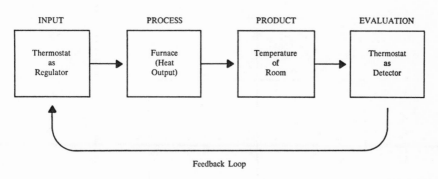

HEATING SYSTEM

INPUT	PROCESS	PRODUCT	EVALUATION
Thermostat as Regulator	Furnace (Heat Output)	Temperature of Room	Thermostat as Detector

Feedback Loop

Figure 1-3

mechanistic, dehumanizing and antithetical to music. However, the systems approach is value free. The misuse or inhumane use of systems can only occur in the hands of the teacher or administrator himself. Humanism can be built into it or left out of it, depending upon how it is applied by humans. The choice of objectives and teaching strategies determines to a large extent whether affective, aesthetic and humanistic learnings will result. If the purpose of the system is to promote human relationships, interests and values, the output should be an effective and efficient humanized system.[4] To be concerned with the learning of each individual child, for example, is certainly humanistic. Nothing is less humanistic than the dull, drilled, large-group approach typical of many music classes.

Critics also argue that technology and associated hardware are dehumanizing because people do not relate to other people in a man/machine learning environment. However there is no basis for claiming that a "live" teacher is more humanistic if there is no meaningful teacher/pupil interaction. Interaction fails to occur when the lecture, discussion or lesson goes over the head of some

---

[4] McManama, *Systems Analysis for Effective School Administration*, p. 180.

BASIC INSTRUCTIONAL SYSTEM FOR ACCOUNTABILITY

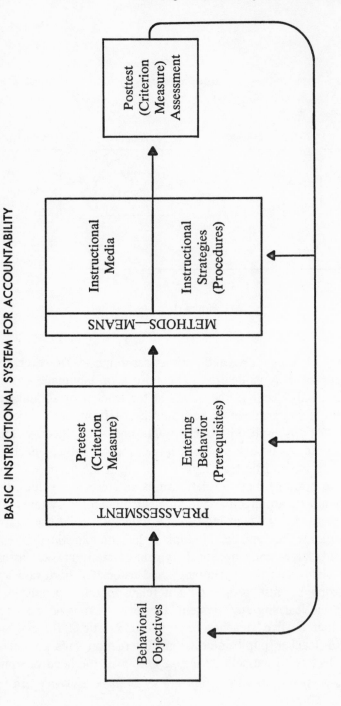

Evaluation Feedback Loop For System Modification

Figure 1-4

students and bores others who know the subject matter. It is more humanistic to provide appropriate instructional media through which the pupil can interact with subject matter at his level of competence. Individualized instruction is the *raison d'etre* of the systems approach.

Another criticism of the systems approach to music teaching involves the behaviorist psychology from which behavioral objectives, behavior modification, performance contracting and related strategies were derived. However an interesting aspect of the cybernetic cycle (Figure 1-2) upon which the systems approach is based is that the various theories of learning can be subsumed under it. It is eclectic in the best sense of the term and quite usable as an empirical basis for teaching. For example, all good teachers use feedback extensively even if only intuitively. Students must know how they are doing in order to learn (i.e., modify their behavior). But the effects of feedback are not limited to response/reinforcement (operant conditioning). They also include such mediating variables as knowledge of results, subsequent decision-making and intelligent action guided by feedback information.

>Whatever one may think of [teacher/pupil] performance contracts, focused on the organization of specific skills, they also are both behavioristic and cognitive. Together, teacher and child work out a plan and follow it with a verbal or written contract that commits the child to work toward his own goal. In their methodology, these contracts focus strictly on behavior and discipline. But the main argument for performance contracts is strictly cognitive: what the child needs is self-confidence—the capacity to feel that he is master of his environment—that is the human development that comes with achievement and social approbation. The greatest of the cognitivists—Johann Heinrich Pestalozzi or Jean Piaget—could not have put better the case for the child-centered approach.
>. . . The school of tomorrow will be neither behavioristic nor cognitive, neither child-centered nor discipline-centered. It will be all of these.
>These old controversies have been phonies all along. We need the behaviorist's triad of practice/reinforcement/feedback to lodge learning in memory [and muscle]. We need

purpose, decision, values and understanding—the cognitive categories, lest learning be mere behavior, activity rather than action.[5]

Organization of the Chapters

We have proposed that accountability is achieved by properly applying the systems approach to music teaching. This provides a positive and optimistic method of improving instruction based upon the proposition that each student shall learn. It provides the proof of results.

This instructional system is a true synthesis. Its parts are interrelated and interacting, and the whole is more than the sum of parts. The difficult task of dissecting the parts for careful examination and analysis is necessary, however. Chapters 2 through 6 are each concerned with a single component of the system. Chapter 2 examines the objectives, and shows how they are derived and written. Chapter 3 discusses preassessment, student entering behavior and competence level. Chapter 4 investigates teaching strategies to achieve objectives. Chapter 5 discusses instructional media. Chapter 6 describes the assessment of student learning and instructional effectiveness.

In Chapter 7 the system is again reassembled. A step-by-step procedure for systems design is presented, followed by specifications for writing a performance contract, and suggestions for managing the instructional system. Appendix A provides actual examples of systematic instruction presently used in music classes in the public school. Sources of educational media are found in Appendix B.

---

[5] Peter Drucker, "School Around the Bend," *Psychology Today*, Vol. 6, No. 1, (June 1972), p. 86. Copyright © Communications/Research/Machines, Inc. Used by permission.

2

writing objectives
for your music classes

Objectives

Upon mastering the content of this chapter, the reader should be able to:

1. Define learning in terms of a change in student behavior.
2. List values and uses of behavioral objectives.
3. List five levels of objectives.
4. Classify outcome statements as goals or objectives.
5. Derive behavioral objectives from general goals.
6. Outline a course of study in behavior/content modules.
7. Write behavioral objectives using the five-point format.
8. Write behavioral objectives with related goal statements.
9. Write a rationale for each objective.

The first step in designing an accountable music program is writing precise statements of behavioral objectives. We must communicate clearly to pupils, colleagues, administrators, parents and *ourselves* what each of our music students will be able to do at the end of instruction that he could not do before. The behavioral objectives should be specified in terms of the important musical tasks that students will learn to perform with appropriate subject-matter content.

Collections of musical objectives are becoming increasingly available from state musical organizations, state departments of education, local school districts and other sources.[1] These statements can be very helpful as models, but they have certain limitations. They must be screened and revised to fit a given local situation. Specific instructional objectives must be derived from them because they are usually written at a higher level of generality. Finally, they do not serve as well to improve instruction and student learning as objectives generated in context by the practicing teacher. All objectives must be tried, evaluated, validated and revised as needed on the basis of the systems approach. This chapter presents the rationale and procedures for deriving and writing instructional objectives for your music classes.

Learning and Student Behavior

When called upon to develop and teach a new class, most teachers sketch out a course of study which consists of some logical order of subject matter. The procedure is helpful for guiding teaching activities and organizing classroom presentations. This has been called the stimulus-oriented approach to instruction. It does not indicate with any degree of certainty what the student is expected to learn. Ralph Tyler summarizes the problem well:

> . . . Learning is a process of acquiring ways of thinking, feeling and acting, that is, acquiring patterns of behavior. A course outline commonly lists the content the course deals

---

[1] California, Kentucky and Michigan have published state-level music objectives. See also *NAEP Music Objectives* (Ann Arbor, Michigan: National Assessment of Educational Progress, 1970).

with, but does not indicate what the student is to learn to do with this content. Is he to memorize it, recognize the principles involved and seek to use the principles in solving problems, or to develop a life-long interest in the subject, or some combination of these and other kinds of behaviors?[2]

Since there are both behavioral and substantive (content) dimensions, a list of subject content alone is not enough. Schools are responsible for developing the competencies of students, not just for the presentation of subject content. In order to learn, the student must process or do something with the information contained in subject matter. Behavioral objectives explicitly specify what is to be done, but they are only implicit in a presentation of content. Without prespecification, they become explicit in the tests that are given. Thus tests become objectives when students do not know what they are expected to do. Think of all the classes you have attended where multiple-choice or true-false tests—not the fancy descriptions in the curriculum guide—were the real goals of the course.

Consider the following example to clarify the notion of the behavior/content module as the basis for course objectives. If an instructor wants to "teach" simple binary form, he must first decide what the student should be able to do (behavior) at the end of instruction to demonstrate that he "knows" the simple binary form (content). The student could *define* it, *identify* it, *describe* it, *diagram* it and/or *compose* it. One possible behavioral objective derived from this analysis utilizes the behavior "to identify:" The student will demonstrate his knowledge of binary form by selecting (i.e., identifying) with 90 percent accuracy the binary forms from the twenty examples and nonexamples provided by the instructor.

Learning is individual—it happens to a learner. It is a change or modification of behavior brought about by experience, training or instruction. When learning is pre-specified as a precise statement of student behavior, it is a behavioral objective. Teachers must be concerned primarily with a student's overt behavior—an observable,

---

[2] Carmen J. Finley and Frances S. Berdie, *The National Assessment Approach to Exercise Development* (Ann Arbor, Michigan: National Assessment of Educational Progress, 1970), p. 11.

measurable action—not covert mental behavior. Learning is inferred from the overt behavior or a product of the behavior. In the former situation, attention is focused upon the behavior itself while it is occurring. The *process* is most important. Rating scales are often used to assess musical behaviors in actual performances. *Products* of behaviors include written exercises, reports and musical compositions.

One major advantage of behavioral objectives is that attention is focused upon the individual learner. In spite of this radical innovation in the classroom, most teachers remain preoccupied with their own performance. They conceive of their jobs as the things they must do and concentrate upon teacher behaviors as lecturing, assigning, conducting, questioning or testing. However the individual student does the learning or he does not learn. It follows that all instruction must be evaluated by the extent to which students achieve course objectives. In this sense there can be no teaching where there has been no learning. This is comparable to the case of the smooth-talking used car salesman who did a great job of selling, but nobody bought anything.

In the accountability approach, learning must be defined as a relatively permanent change in behavior that results from experience or training. The student must respond or act in order to learn. Objectives must be stated in terms of student behavior in order to facilitate and direct learning.

Values of Behavioral Objectives

The trend toward clear statements of performance objectives in all areas of public education is inescapable. The fact that most public school teachers do not write and use them is probably more a failing of their preservice or in-service training than an indictment of the objectives and accountability. There are many values to be gained from the prespecification and use of behavioral objectives.

Objectives clearly communicate the teacher's instructional intent to administrators, school board members, colleagues, parents and lay people. Outcomes are laid out for inspection by all of the interested parties. Your objectives say that you do in fact have a viable music curriculum stated in terms of student exit requirements. Your program is measurable and accountable: you know how you are doing, and you know how the students are doing. Objectives force you to account for each student's learning and present a clear statement of your philosophy of music education at the level of the functioning program.

Objectives provide the teacher with a powerful tool for planning and decision-making. Since objectives specify the behaviors to be performed as a result of instruction, they provide the best indication of appropriate teaching procedures and materials to facilitate learning. They similarly indicate appropriate assessment procedures and assessment items to evaluate student progress and instructional effectiveness. There can be continuous evaluation of each component of the system as well as measurement of the extent of student progress toward objectives.

The most important function of behavioral objectives is to give direction and guidance to students. Objectives clearly communicate the teacher's intent to learners. Students know what they are expected to do to demonstrate achievement. They can evaluate and direct their own learning and know how well they are doing because of continuing feedback or knowledge of results. They can learn at their own rate and choose their own sequence and learning style. Students are spared the time-consuming game of "psyching out" the teacher. They know that tests will truly reflect the performances and content specified in the objectives.

Prespecification of objectives need not eliminate student participation in planning. Flexibility can be built into the system. Additional or alternative objectives can be generated in teacher/pupil planning sessions if time is allocated for that purpose. Furthermore, an accountability program does not lock a teacher into total prespecification. Many authorities suggest that 60 percent of instructional time be devoted to management by objectives, while 40 percent be used for more open-ended activities such as field trips, discussions, humanistic encounters and creative pursuits. Thus objectives can set up minimum standards for all students.

What a student learns *beyond* the minimum level depends upon a number of things, including student capacity, past performance, and the creative flexible involvement of qualified teachers. We should be primarily concerned with *minimizing* individual differences in attainment of valid objectives, and *maximizing* individual differences in the development of higher-level skills, interests, applications, and deeper involvement with a given subject matter.[3]

Eisner has suggested that "expressive objectives" be written to specify an educational encounter without specifying the outcome behavior.[4] This fosters divergent rather than convergent thinking and diversity of learning. Other types of open-ended objectives are called "process" objectives. These are written when a process such as problem solving, creating or discovering is considered more important than a learning product.

Levels of Objectives

Behavioral objectives are small bits of specific learning. When developing objectives for courses we must be certain that they reflect higher-level goals and the values and philosophy of the total school and society. Otherwise, learning will be fragmented and the objectives invalid.

Mention was made earlier of levels of generality of goal and objective statements, and derivation of instructional-level objectives from higher-level goals. To facilitate systematic curriculum design, we can delineate five levels of objectives as they relate to your music classes: educational goals, program goals, course goals, behavioral objectives and test items. Figure 2-1 provides an example of the levels from general to specific.

Educational Goals

The derivation of objectives ideally begins with a statement of goals. Goals at the highest level refer to the broad social outcomes

---

3 William A. Deterline, "Practical Problems in Program Production," in *Programed Instruction*, Phil C. Lang, ed. (NSSE Sixty-sixth Yearbook, Part II, 1967), p. 194.

4 Elliot W. Eisner, "Instructional and Expressive Objectives: Their Formulation and Use in Curriculum," in *Instructional Objectives*, AERA Monograph No. 3 (Chicago: Rand McNally and Company, 1969), pp. 1-31.

LEVELS OF OBJECTIVES

EDUCATIONAL GOAL: The educated person will be able to think creatively.

PROGRAM GOAL: A musically educated person will be musically creative.

COURSE GOAL: The third-grade general music student will be able to create an accompaniment to a song.

BEHAVIORAL OBJECTIVE: Given a prepared melody instrument, the third-grade student will improvise an ostinato to a pentatonic melody.

TEST ITEM: Make up and play an ostinato on the Orff melody bells using two to five notes to accompany a pentatonic song of your choice.

Figure 2-1

of the educational system. They describe the philosophy, broad direction and general purposes of the institution.

These goals filter down to us in a very important way—social values and philosophy set forth priorities. Political and economic realities force choices. With reallocation of resources, some school programs will remain; others will be eliminated or drastically cut back. The music program must find its place within the framework of institutional goals if it is to receive institutional support.

Program Goals

Program goals describe in broad terms the direction the music program should take to achieve the goals of the school. Valid program goals establish the music program as a part of general education.

Many states are now in the process of deriving and validating program goals, including goals for music. State-level objectives establish programs that, at the very least, should be available to every student. These broad objectives, when endorsed by the state department of education, firmly establish music as a required part of the total school curriculum. This is encouraging. It is no longer enough that administrators endorse music at their national meetings, when local realities and priorities force music from many local school programs.

Thus the first step in writing your objectives is to consider the long-range educational values and goals of your courses. Write down in general terms "where" and "how" each course fits into the total school program and philosophy. This is essential since all lower-level objectives are derived from and/or validated with reference to higher-level goals.

Course Goals

The next step is to note the broad aims and purposes of your course. Course goals should state in general terms what a student should know and understand; what skills and techniques he should have; and what he might be expected to appreciate, value or like as a result of your course. These are the important capabilities or competencies you want your students to develop.

An intensive study of subject matter content is appropriate here as a source of goals. Music as a discipline offers *many* potential learning goals. Curriculum guides, course outlines, textbooks, method books, tests and final examinations all provide sources of possible course content. Students' suggestions and interests can be utilized. Tradition, society and culture are a source. Journals, research findings and the latest practices advocated by authorities provide additional sources. Ultimately, you must decide what is appropriate for your course. Since students cannot learn everything about a subject area, you must select what is most essential and useful. Be particularly concerned with affective learnings. Feelings, attitudes, preferences and appreciations are important outcomes of any music program.

Behavioral Objectives

It follows that the general statements we use when we describe subject matter must be restated in operational (behavioral) terms. What are the behavioral indicators of goal attainment? What does a student look like or what is he doing when he is understanding and appreciating? A performance objective consists of a description of each individual learner's behavior when he is processing information contained within subject matter. The learner must be capable of doing something with aspects of subject matter content.

Thus the basic component of the behavioral objective consists of a behavior/content module. The learner can do something with the musical phenemenon with which he is interacting. He *sings* a *pentatonic melody;* he *plays* a *rhythm pattern;* he *identifies* a *ternary form.* Although these illustrations are simplistic, this notion is central to writing behavioral objectives.

The next section investigates in detail the process of writing behavioral objectives; however, an outline is included here as an overview. A well-constructed behavioral objective, stated completely, requires a five-part operational structure: 1) subject (characteristic student), 2) action verb (observable, measurable behavior), 3) object (course content), 4) conditions (facilitating or limiting) and 5) criteria (performance standards). (See Figure 2-2.) Behavioral objectives tell explicitly what the learner will do at the end of instruction that he could not do before. It is a "terminal" performance in this sense.[5]

A task analysis of the objective will indicate if it can be achieved independently in one or two learning episodes, or if it will require the acquisition of several subobjectives for mastery. The latter is more frequently the case. The terminal objective (major task) must be analyzed to determine appropriate subobjectives (subtasks that lead to the major task. Subobjectives are often described as "enabling objectives," "enroute objectives" or "dependencies." Derive them by asking such questions as: What must the learner be able to do before he can reach the terminal objective? What concepts and competencies must he possess?[6]

Test Items

The fifth level of objectives consists of the specific test items that you will accept as evidence that learning has occurred. These test items should be constructed at the same time that behavioral objectives are written. Each test item must correspond directly to its objective. Behavioral objectives do not always provide a test, but they do imply the types of test items that are appropriate to sample student achievement. Test items clarify and sharpen behavioral objectives. The better an objective is written, the more it will resemble a test item. This is especially true of objectives in the psychomotor domain. The process quickly exposes objectives that cannot be evaluated. Conversely, it eliminates potential test items that are irrelevant to objectives.

The pool of test items is assembled to form a "criterion-referenced test." This method of construction should result in a test with

---

[5]   Robert F. Mager, *Preparing Instructional Objectives* (Belmont, California: Fearon Publishers, 1962).

[6]   See Robert M. Gagné, *The Conditions of Learning,* 2nd ed. (New York: Holt, Reinhart and Winston, Inc., 1970) for a detailed analysis.

high content validity if there is at least one test item for every objective. The test corresponds on a one-to-one basis with objectives. As discussed later, two versions of this test should be used for pretesting and posttesting.

There is another reason to concentrate upon test items. Think about the courses you have taken. From the student's point of view, tests indicate the real objectives of a course. Students study for tests, not for any stated objectives, especially if grades are given. Thus one way to capitalize on this potent motivating force is to present your objectives as test items. Many successful teachers distribute rating scales and tests as statements of their objectives.

Finally, remember that testing is not limited to paper-and-pencil activities. Playing, singing, pointing and demonstrating are observable test behaviors. See Chapters 3 and 6 for a complete discussion of tests and evaluation.

Writing Behavioral Objectives

An educational "goal" is a broad, general statement of direction and purpose. An "objective" is a specific, desired accomplishment that can be, in addition, measured within a given period of time. The latter is used for accountability and assessment. It has been called by many names (no humor intended): "behavioral objective," "performance objective," "instructional objective," "learning objective" and even "course objective."

The term "behavioral" has negative connotations for many music educators because of the link to behavioral psychology. However the notion that overt behavior is the only acceptable indication of learning need not be tied to any single psychological theory. As suggested in Chapter 1, the systems approach and the cybernetic cycle are value free, eclectic and quite usable in music teaching.

The term "performance objective" may appeal most to musicians and certainly connotes appropriate applicability. The procedures used in many music classes have been held up as an example of good teaching since the days of progressive education. However, the idea that performance only refers to singing, playing, moving, listening and creating (the old five-fold curriculum) is misleading.

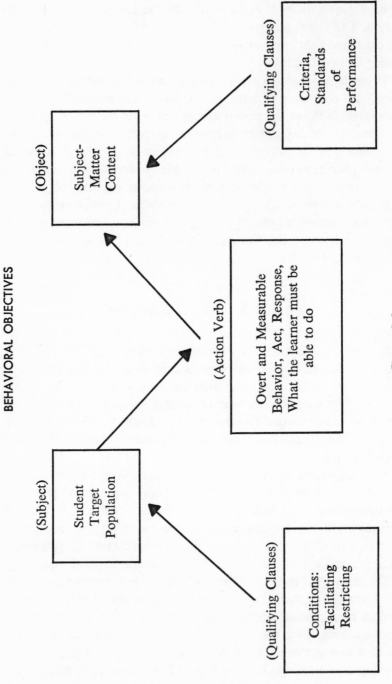

BEHAVIORAL OBJECTIVES

(Object)
Subject-Matter Content

(Qualifying Clauses)
Criteria, Standards of Performance

(Action Verb)
Overt and Measurable Behavior, Act, Response, What the learner must be able to do

(Subject)
Student Target Population

(Qualifying Clauses)
Conditions: Facilitating Restricting

Figure 2-2

For example, I have heard many music teachers argue that "our activities are our objectives." This is only a half-truth and certainly a confusion of means and ends. Furthermore, objectives as activities are more appropriate for group outcomes—they are helpful for evaluating the performances of ensembles. The adjudicators' rating scale is a good example. Objectives for the individual student, even if presented in group situations, specify what each individual, not just the group, will be able to do.

Whatever you choose to call your objectives, the format will identify student exit requirements in behavioral terms. The behavior/content module was suggested as a way to begin the writing task. However, a well-formulated, completely stated behavioral objective consists of the five-part operational structure presented in Figure 2-2: learner description; observable, measurable behavior; subject matter content; conditions; and criteria. For clarity of derivation and use, the objective can be related to its broad, nonbehavioral goal statement. Finally, a rationale or justification can be appended to help assure student commitment. Figure 2-3 provides concrete illustrations to which you can frequently refer as you read. Follow the chart horizontally for instant objectives.

Learner Description

The subject of a behavioral statement specifies the characteristic student from the target population to which the objective is addressed. He or she can be described in terms of grade level, course type, or student group. Any phrase that describes the learner can be appropriate: the third-grade general music student, the junior high school choir member, or the high school band member.

Observable Behavior and Content Reference

Action verbs are used to write behavioral objectives. They must be unequivocal in interpretation if objectives are to clearly communicate intent. Behavior in this sense is an observable, measurable action or a product of the action, and not an internal state. The covert changes are inferred from the overt behavior. To love music,

INSTANT MUSICAL OBJECTIVES CHART

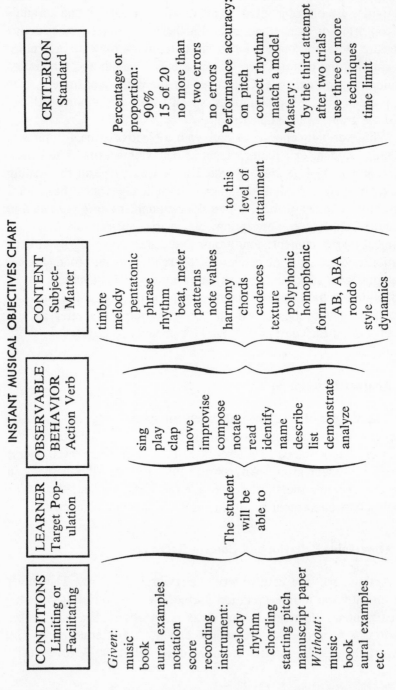

CONDITIONS Limiting or Facilitating	LEARNER Target Population	OBSERVABLE BEHAVIOR Action Verb	CONTENT Subject-Matter	CRITERION Standard
Given: music book aural examples notation score recording instrument: melody rhythm chording starting pitch manuscript paper *Without:* music book aural examples etc.	The student will be able to	sing play clap move improvise compose notate read identify name describe list demonstrate analyze	timbre melody pentatonic phrase rhythm beat, meter patterns note values harmony chords cadences texture polyphonic homophonic form AB, ABA rondo style dynamics	Percentage or proportion: 90% 15 of 20 no more than two errors no errors Performance accuracy: on pitch correct rhythm match a model Mastery: by the third attempt after two trials use three or more techniques time limit

to this level of attainment

Figure 2-3

to appreciate it, know about it, and really understand it are all goals that have much merit. However, they are impossible to assess in terms of student performance. What does a student do when he really understands music? We need some indicators of this understanding similar to the following behavioral outcome in which the action verb "identify" is used: The student will demonstrate his understanding of musical style by correctly identifying nine of ten examples played by the instructor from the Renaissance through contemporary periods.

Many action verbs are part of the vocabulary of a functioning musical subject content; e.g., sing, play, move, improvise, notate, read (notation), analyze (music), compose and create. In addition to the direct, disciplinary approach, music teachers can take advantage of classification schemes developed by curriculum specialists and researchers. Objectives have been categorized by domain—cognitive, psychomotor and affective—and by level from simple to complex in taxonomies and learning hierarchies.[7] Using these guides, you can make certain that your objectives collectively represent a balanced program encompassing all levels of learning. A cautionary note must be inserted here. Figure 2-4 illustrates the interrelationships of the domains and the danger of exclusive and artificial separation. Many authorities insist that the "domains" constitute an existential unity. For example, students learn subject content (knowledge) as they do something with it (skill). In the same process, they learn to like or dislike it (attitude). Yet the objectives you write will tend to emphasize one or another of the behavior types. Cognitive objectives emphasize thinking and mental processes; psychomotor objectives emphasize skill and technique;

---

[7] Benjamin S. Bloom, et al., Taxonomy of Educational Objectives, Handbook I: Cognitive Domain (New York: David McKay Co., Inc., 1965).
David R. Krathwohl, et al., Taxonomy of Educational Objectives, Handbook II: Affective Domain (New York: David McKay Co., Inc., 1964).
Elizabeth Jane Simpson, The Classification of Educational Objectives: Psychomotor Domain (Urbana: University of Illinois, 1966).
Richard W. Burns, New Approaches to Behavioral Objectives (Dubuque, Iowa: Wm. C. Brown, 1972), pp. 22-36.
Sidney J. Drumheller, Handbook of Curriculum Design for Individualized Instruction: A Systems Approach (Englewood Cliffs, N.J.: Educational Technology Publications, Inc., 1971).
Gagne, The Conditions of Learning.

THE INTERRELATIONSHIP OF DOMAINS

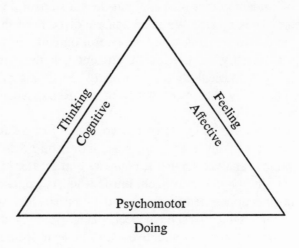

Figure 2-4

and affective objectives emphasize feelings, attitudes and appreciation.

Five categories of verbs have been delineated from current research by Gerlach and Ely for objectives in the cognitive domain.[8] They can be adapted to the cognitive content of any subject area. They are listed here with some illustrative musical content references to form behavior/content modules.

1. Identify—discriminate between (high-low, soft-loud, fast-slow, etc.); classify (instruments by families, musical types, forms, etc.); categorize (aural examples of styles); recognize; select; mark; match; point out

2. Name—list (instruments of the orchestra, musical elements); label (families of instruments, lines and spaces on the staff): give (examples of forms, compositions); state (names and dates of major style periods)

---

8   Vernon S. Gerlach and Donald P. Ely, *Teaching and Media: A Systems Approach* (Englewood Cliffs, N. J.: Prentice-Hall, Inc., 1971), pp. 79-85.

3. Describe—define (musical terms); explain (musical trends, developments); tell how (to construct a triad, interpet a meter signature and key signature); analyze (a composition); give examples of (styles); demonstrate; perform the steps
4. Order—list in sequence (the historical styles); rank (the musical performances); arrange in sequence (the flats and sharps or cycle of fifths)
5. Construct—compose (ternary form); notate (a composition); prepare (for performance); arrange (for four voices); create; make; build; write; draw.

Most objectives in the psychomotor domain involve musical performance skills or techniques. Some verbs and content references follow: Perform (music); sing (a song); play (a musical instrument); move (to rhythm); improvise (upon a given chord progression); read (notation); assemble (a musical instrument).

Verbs utilized in statements of affective objectives describe an observable behavior from which an attitude, aesthetic response, preference or interest can be inferred. The best method of evaluating affective objectives is through informal observation. The critical question is not if the student *can* do something, but if he *will* do it under appropriate circumstances. Therefore, appropriate verbs specify "approach" behavior of varying degrees of intensity as contrasted to "avoidance" behavior.[9] Here are some indicators of approach behaviors—participates (in performance groups); responds to (music); prizes; willingly participates; demonstrates preference; seeks (musical information and activities); initiates; values; consistently demonstrates preference; elects (music classes); attends (musical functions on his own time).

Conditions

A well-written objective includes the limiting or facilitating conditions under which the student is to perform. A modifying clause

---

9   Robert F. Mager, *Developing Attitude Toward Learning* (Palo Alto, Calif.: Fearon Publishers, 1968).

specifies the materials, equipment or other aids the learner may use, or it indicates the restrictions imposed upon his terminal performance. Here are some clauses that indicate conditions:

Given. . .	Without. . .
Provided with. . .	Restricted from. . .
With the aid of. . .	Without the aid of. . .

Conditions should be relevant, not redundant. Do not belabor the obvious. If the intent is clear, you can omit these clauses from your objectives.

Criterion

The next important component of a behavioral objective is the standard of performance. How well is the learner expected to perform? To what extent is he expected to achieve? The criterion can be stated in terms of the number, percentage of proportion of test items that must be correctly answered or executed; e.g., no errors, no more than two errors, 90 percent correct. The criterion can also be stated in terms of time limit; e.g., within ten minutes. It can be stated in terms of skill criteria, performance accuracy or correspondence to a model; e.g., holding a steady beat, singing on pitch, or performing correct rhythm patterns. Finally, it can be stated in terms of mastery; e.g., achieve by the third attempt, or use all of the principles. Evaluation should be as objective as possible; thus, the standards should be clearly stated.

Relating Objectives to Broad Nonbehavioral Goals

Many music teachers resist writing their own behavioral objectives or using the musical objectives adopted by their school system. They feel that the long, prescriptive lists of specifics impede instruction rather than improve it. They prefer broad goals and general principles to guide their teaching, instead of overprecise details and seemingly endless paper work. They further point out the danger of breaking up musical content into little behavioral pieces that may not add up to the important goals we seek in music education.

The resistance and conflict generated by the goals-versus-objectives debate can best be arbitrated by a merger. Burns has suggested that specifically defined behavioral objectives can be more usable if they are related to the broadly stated nonbehavioral goal from which they were derived.[10] The following statement illustrates how the merger can be effected. The first part presents a goal, while the second part specifies a behavioral description or indicator. "The music appreciation student will develop an understanding of musical form so that he can identify with 85% accuracy the binary, ternary and rondo forms in the examples played by the instructor."

Providing a Rationale

Learners, too, may resist behavioral objectives if they cannot find personal value in them. Teachers may know the reasons that students should study to achieve objectives. However, students will not work toward objectives to which they are not committed any more than teachers will teach toward objectives to which they are not committed. According to Canfield, objectives should be explained and defended, not merely presented.[11] Teachers should include a statement of rationale or justification with each objective to explain its importance to the learner. Thus a complete statement would consist of a goal, behavioral objective and rationale.

GOAL—The student will know the historical styles of the music he hears.
BEHAVIORAL OBJECTIVE—Upon hearing musical examples characteristic of the major historical style periods, the student will identify the period with at least 85% accuracy.

---

[10] Richard W. Burns, "The Theory of Expressing Objectives," *Educational Technology*, VII (October 30, 1967), pp. 1-3.

[11] Albert A. Canfield, "A Rationale for Performance Objectives," *Audiovisual Instruction*, 13 (February, 1968), p. 128.

RATIONALE—If you know the major historical style periods, you will become a better listener and performer. Recognizing styles helps you appreciate serious music. It provides you with the basis for a valid interpretation of the music you play.

The idea is to generate learner interest and effort. Objectives written at the vocabulary level of the students will serve better for guidance and commitment, especially when a statement of rationale is included.

Self-Check Mastery Test

A mastery test is provided at the end of each chapter to help you determine if you have reached the objectives. Some answers are included with the test. The others can be found under their corresponding chapter subheadings. Check yourself before proceeding and review if necessary.

1. What does "learning" mean in an accountable music program?
2. What are the values and uses of behavioral objectives?
3. What are the five levels of objectives?
4. Which of the following are goals (G)? Which are behavorial objectives (BO)?
   a. The student will appreciate music.
   b. Given a chording instrument and appropriate music, the student will play an accompaniment to a two-chord song with no more than one chord-choice error.
   c. Upon hearing musical examples characteristic of the major historical styles, the student will identify each example as Renaissance, Baroque, Classical, Romantic or Contemporary with 90 percent accuracy.
   d. Upon hearing several appropriate examples, the student will know that program music is inspired by nonmusical ideas.
   e. Given a familiar song and a starting tone, the student

       will sing the song on pitch.

    f. Given ten aural examples of major and minor triads, the student will identify each as either major or minor.

    g. Given patterns of quarter and eighth notes, the student will understand how to accurately read the rhythmic notation.

    h. Given a series of aural phrases, the student will indicate points of relative repose (cadence).

5. What are objectives that can lead to the following goals?

    a. The (lower elementary level) student will sing musically.

    b. The (upper elementary level) student will be musically creative.

6. What are possible behavior/content modules for a course you are teaching? Write up a complete course if possible.

7. What are several objectives you can use in a course you are teaching? Write them using the five-point format.

8. Include a goal statement with each objective in question 7.

9. Write a rationale for each objective in question 7.

Answers For Questions 4 and 5

4. a. G, b. BO, c. BO, d. G, e. BO, f. BO, g. G, h. BO

5. a. Sample objectives leading to the goal (singing):

   (1) Given a pitch within his range, the student will match the pitch vocally

   (2) Given short tonal patterns within his range, the student will imitate the patterns with accurate pitch.

   (3) The student will sing simple melodies by imitation.

   (4) The student will use appropriate phrasing while singing a song.

    b. Sample objectives leading to the goal (musical creativity):

   (1) The student will freely respond to musical stimuli through bodily movement.

   (2) The student will improvise on classroom instruments.

(3) The student will improvise (and perhaps notate) rhythmic patterns.

(4) The student will make up (create or improvise) vocal and instrumental *ostinati* to given melodies.

(5) The student will make up (create or improvise) a musical "composition" using sound sources available in the classroom such as body sounds, wastebaskets, pencils, etc.

(6) The student will make up (create) a musical composition or accompaniment using a tape recorder and sound distortion.

(7) The student will create and notate a musical composition employing classroom sounds, rhythm instruments, tape recorders and/or orchestral instruments.

3

preassessing your music students

Objectives

Upon mastering the content of this chapter the reader should be able to:

1. Describe the function of the pretest.
2. List and briefly describe the four categories of musical objectives used for assessment.
3. Classify musical objectives in the appropriate category.
4. List appropriate modes of evaluation for each category.
5. Describe the function of the entry test.
6. Analyze a terminal objective to derive a sequential structure of subobjectives.

Educators have talked about individual differences for a long time, but nothing much seems to be done about learner differences in the classroom. We tend to teach as if all students were alike. We assume too much about their background, experience, initial competence, learning rate and learning style. However, we must ascertain where each student is now if we expect him to attain the instructional objectives.

Preassessment is often called "needs assessment." It provides information about what a student needs to learn. Given test results, we can analyze student needs and prescribe the course of his learning. Specifically, preassessment answers two important instructional questions: 1) Can the student already achieve the objectives we plan to teach? 2) Does the student possess the prerequisite learnings needed to achieve the objectives? To answer the first question a pretest is given. As discussed in the next section, the pretest is iden'ical or parallel to the posttest (sometimes called an exit test). To answer the second question an entry test is given. Entry tests assess prerequisite knowledge and abilities to determine if the student is ready to undertake the learning tasks.

Pretests

In Chapter 2, you were instructed to write test items at the same time you developed objectives. Test items are the specific performances that you will accept as evidence that learning has occurred (i.e., your objectives have been achieved by the student). You compile these test items that correspond directly to objectives to form a criterion-referenced test. Although the primary function of the criterion test is that of a posttest (exit test or end-of-unit measure), a form of the criterion test should be used as a pretest to determine which of the instructional objectives the learner can already attain prior to instruction. You can use a parallel test form or the identical test. The parallel form is possible to construct if enough criterion items are generated for each objective. You then have two different tests to assess the same set of objectives. A simpler approach is to give the posttest—in which case the pretest and posttests are identical. You literally give the final exam before instruction begins.

Pretesting can help create interest in the topic to be studied. It is certainly an excellent way to present and clarify objectives. Care must be taken that the formal pretest does not discourage or frustrate the student. A thorough explanation of its diagnostic purpose will help prevent negative attitudes from forming. Tell students that these tests do not affect their grades. Ask them to peruse the test before attempting to answer the questions to determine if they feel that they can successfully complete it. If they cannot, advise them not to try but proceed to the learning tasks.

Perhaps an informal pretest may suit your purposes better. Certainly you can observe performance, discuss the topic, and question students informally about the unit to be mastered. This is often more stimulating than a formal pretest and it can also serve the purpose of clarifying objectives.

The purpose of all testing in the systems model is to analyze the present level of performance of each student and to prescribe appropriate new learning tasks. The process is expressed in this formula: proposed learning, minus pretest competence, equals needed learning. Pretesting allows the student to move ahead to the learning that he needs. Valuable class time is not wasted going over what he already knows. There is no more going through a method book lesson by lesson in a lock-step progression. Students will not be bored or become discipline problems. They can go ahead and do the things we made them wait for before. They will not be admonished, "No, you can't do that now. We will get to it next week (or next semester)."

The method of developing pretests and posttests is described in detail in Chapter 6. The following programed material presents a "crash course" in categorizing your objectives for assessment and constructing appropriate test items. It further illustrates an important value of programed instruction—quick mastery when needed.

Scan the exit test before you begin. If you think you know the answers, take the exit test as a pretest. Check your answers. Read the program and retake the test if you miss any questions.

CATEGORIZING AND ASSESSING MUSICAL OBJECTIVES

A Short Program

OBJECTIVES OF THE PROGRAM

When you have completed this program, you should be able to:

1. list and briefly describe the four categories of musical objectives for assessment purposes.
2. classify musical objectives in the appropriate category.
3. list appropriate modes of evaluation for each category.

The program will describe each category of objectives, present examples and help you determine appropriate types of assessment questions for each.

INSTRUCTIONS	Answer Column
Use a card or paper to cover answers in the answer column.	Cover answers until you have selected or written your choice.
Select or write your answer in the space provided. Confirm your answer by sliding card to expose answer.	
Sample Item:	
You *want* to learn how to classify musical objectives.	
Yes/No (circle yes) (now confirm your answer)	Yes

SET ONE	
Four Categories of Objectives	Answer Column
1. Musical objectives can be classified into four categories. The method of testing the	

objective will determine the appropriate category. If an objective can be tested completely with a paper and pencil test, it is a KNOWLEDGE objective. Such objectives are about musical information.

"The student will identify musical instruments by name upon seeing them." Is this a KNOWLEDGE objective? Yes/No	Yes
"The student will properly attach the reed to the mouthpiece." Is this a KNOWLEDGE objective? Yes/No	No
	(Motor performance objective)

2. AURAL PERCEPTION objectives require the student to *listen* to something during the testing of the objective.

"The student will list six major composers of the Romantic era." Is this an AURAL PERCEPTION objective? Yes/No	No (Knowledge)
"The student will identify the historical style of the musical compositions he hears." Is this an AURAL PERCEPTION objective? Yes/No	Yes

3. MOTOR PERFORMANCE objectives require the student to physically respond (sing, play, clap, read music, etc.) during the test as a way of applying what he has learned.

"The student will clap rhythmic patterns notated on the chalk board." Is this an example of a MOTOR PERFORMANCE objective? Yes/No	Yes
"The student will play the autoharp to accompany his singing." Is this a MOTOR PERFORMANCE objective? Yes/No	Yes

4. AFFECTIVE objectives encompass feelings, attitudes and preferences. "The student will pursue music outside of school." Is this an AFFECTIVE objective? Yes/No "The student will tolerate new ideas, techniques and musical styles." Is this an AFFECTIVE objective? Yes/No	Yes Yes
5. Summary of categories: a. Objectives involving musical information are............ objectives. b. Objectives requiring listening to music and applying knowledge are....... ....objectives. c. Objectives requiring the application of knowledge through physical response are......... .... objectives. d. Objectives involving attitudes, preferences and feelings are............. objectives.	Knowledge Aural Perception Motor Performance Affective

SET TWO

Appropriate Tests

1. KNOWLEDGE, especially memory, is easy to test, even in a large group situation. Use a paper and pencil format for the verbal or symbolic responses. For example, multiple-choice questions are objective and easy to grade. A constructed response test, like the following illustration, is also appropriate.

> EXAMPLE OF KNOWLEDGE OBJECTIVE AND TEST ITEM
> *Objective*: Given a list of composers, the student will identify the major historical style period in which each composed (85 percent accuracy required).

> *Sample Item*: On the line preceding the name of each composer write the historical style period in which he composed.
> ....Mozart ....Wagner
> ....Brahms ....Stravinsky
> ....Bach ....Haydn

Which of the tests listed below are most suitable for assessing attainment of KNOWLEDGE objectives?

a.	True-false test Yes/No	Yes
b.	Multiple-choice test Yes/No	Yes
c.	Completion test Yes/No	Yes
d.	Rating scale of performance Yes/No	No
e.	Essay test Yes/No	Yes
f.	Student reports Yes/No	Yes
g.	Informal observation Yes/No	No

2. Assessment of AURAL PERCEPTION objectives is similar to knowledge objectives. Paper and pencil format is appropriate. However, to assess AURAL PERCEPTION objectives you must also have a(n)........ ....

aural stimulus (musical example or sound source)

3. Which of the following tests are suitable for assessing AURAL PERCEPTION objectives?

a. Recording is played and students answer multiple-choice items, identifying instruments that are performing. Yes/No

Yes

b. Students write chord progressions from Roman numerals. Yes/No

No

c. Students match the name of a composition with its composer. Yes/No

No

d. Students classify music they hear by writing the historical period in which it was composed. Yes/No

Yes

e. Students choose the given musical notation that matches the music they
hear.   Yes/No   Yes

---

4. MOTOR PERFORMANCE objectives require assessment through individual testing,
although individuals can sometimes be assessed in a group setting. Which of the following tests and evaluating techniques are
appropriate for assessing MOTOR PER-
FORMANCE objectives?
    a. Multiple-choice test of musical no-
       tation.   Yes/No   No
    b. Adjudicators form.   Yes/No   Yes
                                                               (solo form)
    c. Teacher-made rating scale. Yes/No   Yes
    d. Playing a recording and asking stu-
       dents to pick out mistakes. Yes/No   No
    e. Informal observation.   Yes/No   Yes
    f. Check list.   Yes/No   Yes
    g. Tape recording a rehearsal to pick
       out individual mistakes.   Yes/No   Yes
    h. Video tape recording.   Yes/No   Yes

---

5. AFFECTIVE objectives are considered by
many to be the most important outcomes of
the music program. Yet they are the most
difficult to assess. Effective tests must be
"nonreactive." That is, students should not
know they are being "tested." Which of the
following assessment methods are appropriate for testing AFFECTIVE objectives?
    a. Have the student write an essay:
       "What I Like About My Music
       Class."   Yes/No   No
                                                               (reactive)
    b. Informally observe if student responds
       favorably, enthusiastically, or other-
       wise. Yes/No   Yes

c. Tape record without student's knowledge to find out his preferences. Yes/No	Yes
d. Determine student's out-of-school musical activities by use of a check list, log or activity inventory. Yes/No	Yes
e. Determine preferences by noting in a log book what student does. Yes/No	Yes

Summary of Appropriate Tests
List appropriate types of tests for each category.

a. KNOWLEDGE objectives	Objective test (true-false, multiple-choice, etc.), essay, completion, student reports.
b. AURAL PERCEPTION objectives	Listening tests with any objective test mode.
c. MOTOR PERFORMANCE objectives	Informal observation, rating scales, check lists, VTR.
d. AFFECTIVE objectives	Nonreactive observational techniques, anecdotal records, logs, activity inventory.

EXIT TEST FOR THE PROGRAM

Categorizing and Assessing Musical Objectives

I. List and briefly describe the four categories of musical objectives for assessment purposes.
A.
B.
C.
D.

II. Classify each behavioral objective for testing purposes as:
A. a knowledge objective

  B. an aural-perception objective

  C. a motor-application objective

  D. an affective objective

by circling the correct designation for each of the numbered behavioral objectives that follow.

A B C D (1) Given rhythmic patterns of quarter and eighth notes, the student will clap them with no errors.

A B C D (2) Given recorded musical examples, the student will be able to recognize meters that move in groups of twos and threes.

A B C D (3) Given a list of music he has heard, the student will indicate his musical preferences.

A B C D (4) Given the rhythmic symbol and rests (𝅝 𝅗𝅥. 𝅘𝅥 𝅘𝅥 𝅘𝅥𝅮 ▬ 𝄽 𝄾), the student will write the name of each with no errors.

A B C D (5) Given a rhythm instrument the student will maintain a steady beat.

A B C D (6) Given recorded musical examples of pairs of pitches which are same or different, the pupil will identify them verbally as *same* or *different*.

A B C D (7) Given a staff and the notes of a chromatic scale, the pupil will arrange them in a tone row.

A B C D (8) Given recorded examples of program music, the student will voluntarily indicate a personal preference for one of the compositions.

A B C D (9) Given a familiar song and a starting tone, the student will sing the song on pitch.

A B C D (10) The student will list the major historical periods in chronological order and include at least three major composers with each period.

III. List appropriate types of tests for each of the categories.

  A. knowledge objectives

  B. aural perception objectives

  C. motor performance objectives

  D. affective objectives

ANSWERS

I.   A.   Knowledge objectives consist of musical information that can be assessed with paper and pencil tests.
B.   Aural perception objectives require listening to music and applying knowledge.
C.   Motor performance objectives require an application of knowledge through a physical response.
D.   Affective objectives. encompass attitudes, feelings and preferences.

II.   (1) C, (2) B, (3) D, (4) A, (5) C, (6) B, (7) A, (8) D, (9) C, (10) A

III.   A.   Knowledge objectives—objective tests, essay tests, completion tests, student reports
B.   Aural perception objectives—listening tests with any objective test mode
C.   Motor performance objectives—informal observation, rating scales, check lists.
D.   Affective objectives—nonreactive observational techniques such as activity inventories, logs, and anecdotal records.

Entry Tests

In a broad sense, "entering behavior" includes all of the personal learning characteristics that a student brings with him into class: his level of maturity, readiness, aptitude, achievement level, intelligence, motor acuity and interests. Standardized tests provide certain types of information relative to most of these academic constructs. More is said about this in Chapter 6. The use of the term "entering behavior" in systems design helps clarify the meaning of the functionally ambiguous terms listed above. Entering behavior simply refers to the prerequisite competencies needed to attain the instructional objectives. It follows that entry tests must be developed to ascertain the presence or absence of essential prerequisite knowledge and abilities.

Like the pretest, the entry test need not be limited to paper-and-pencil activities. You can informally discuss the proposed learning unit with students and ask questions about their present levels of accomplishment. You can observe their performance to see if they are ready to tackle the new task. The "tryout" is a good example that has been used in music teaching for years.

Entry tests indicate what remedial instruction or review is needed before instruction can begin. You can use programed materials, individual tutoring, games, workbooks, reference books or perhaps a review with the entire class to facilitate remedial learning.

The notion of prerequisites assumes that objectives are hierarchically ordered or sequenced to progress toward terminal goals. The rationale for having prerequisite courses and learnings is based upon this assumption. Thus entry testing is closely related to the sequencing of objectives and the analysis of terminal objectives into subobjectives. The acquisition of a subobjective becomes the entry level for the next higher objective. The exit test for one unit becomes the entry test for the next unit of instruction.

Organizing and Ordering Objectives

Much has been written about learning sequence, objective analysis, task analysis, and the hierarchical structure of a well-prepared instructional system.[1] Most of the information, however, remains theoretical, empirically untested, and directed to easily sequenced subject areas as science or mathematics. This section presents a simplified method for ordering your musical objectives.

The first important step for sequencing instruction is to develop a set of well-stated objectives. We have seen that the use of behavioral objectives has reversed the emphasis from teacher activities to student learning. In a similar way the emphasis in sequencing has been shifted from the order of presentation of subject matter to

[1] Leslie J. Briggs, *Sequencing of Instruction In Relation to Hierarchies of Competence* (Pittsburgh: American Institutes for Research, 1968).
Drumheller, *Handbook of Curriculum Design for Individualized Instruction.*
Gagné, *The Conditions of Learning,* pp. 237-276.
W. James Popham and Eva L. Baker, *Planning an Instructional Sequence* (Englewood Cliffs, N.J.: Prentice-Hall, Inc., 1970), pp. 43-61.
Paul A. Twelker, "Designing Instructional Systems," from *CORD, National Research Training Manual,* Jack Crawford, ed. (Monmouth, Oregon: Teaching Research Division, Oregon State System of Higher Education), pp. II 2-20.

the optimal order of student learning. Can you determine if there is an optimal order in which your objectives should be presented to facilitate student learning? Which objectives are dependent upon the acquisition of other objectives? Which objectives are independent and complete in themselves? Usually you must move back from each terminal objective by means of task analysis to determine what subobjectives must be mastered in order to achieve the terminal objective. Thus organization is derived from a process of sequencing and analyzing. (See Figure 3-1.)

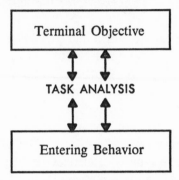

Figure 3-1

Like any problem-solving process, the hierarchy of enabling objectives may not present itself neatly during your first attempts at sequencing and analyzing. As is implied in the terms, there may be a working forward (sequencing) and a working backward (analyzing). As the structure develops holes may need to be filled and extraneous objectives may need to be discarded.

An analysis of listed objectives indicates which objectives are dependent upon others. Sequence is critical here because the mastery of dependencies facilitates the learning of higher-level objectives. If an objective is independent of others it can be taught at any time in the instructional period.

Starting with a terminal objective, you base the sequence on an analysis of the task or tasks specified in the performance. What must a student be able to do before he can master the objective? Task analysis results in an inferred, tentative hierarchy of learning. That is, you begin with this plausible sequence of instruction that must be validated through empirical classroom trials with the students for whom it was designed.

The hierarchy of tasks begins with the complex terminal performance and proceeds down in layers to simpler tasks. To assure the acquisition of each essential competency, the tasks at each level should be mastered before moving up to the next level. The process exposes irrelevant and extraneous objectives that may derive from the logical and traditional ordering of subject content. At this point you can separate content into "need to know" and "nice to know" categories. Considering both the behavioral and the content dimensions jointly simplifies the selection of critical subobjectives. The "nice to knows" are not necessary for the mastery of terminal performance.

Figure 3-2 is an example of a hierarchical structure that resulted from the analysis of a terminal objective for a unit of programed instruction in musical form. Working backward using the question, "What must the student know or be able to do to accomplish the objective?" we find that a student must be able to identify a "period" and distinguish similar and contrasting phrases. To identify a period he must know the effects of cadences (complete and incomplete) and the type of cadences that give these effects. He must also be able to identify a phrase.

In the actual development of this material it was assumed that the student could read music and had some elementary background in music theory. An entry test was used to verify this. Note that the terminal objective of this unit is an enabling objective for learning higher-level forms.[2]

Objectives involving "motives" and "symmetry of formal design" traditionally found in content presentations were deleted after analysis because they were irrelevant to the terminal objective. They were in the logical content sequence but at this point they were "nice to know" objectives, not "need to know" objectives in the learning sequence.

The following steps presented by Paul Twelker in the *CORD National Research Training Manual*[3] summarize the discussion well.

---

[2] This illustrates the semantic difficulty that results from the phrase, "terminal objective." Since most behavioral objectives lead somewhere beyond themselves, they are only terminal to a specific instructional sequence. Asahal Woodruff has quipped that the only terminal objective that he will accept is death.

[3] pp. II 19-20.

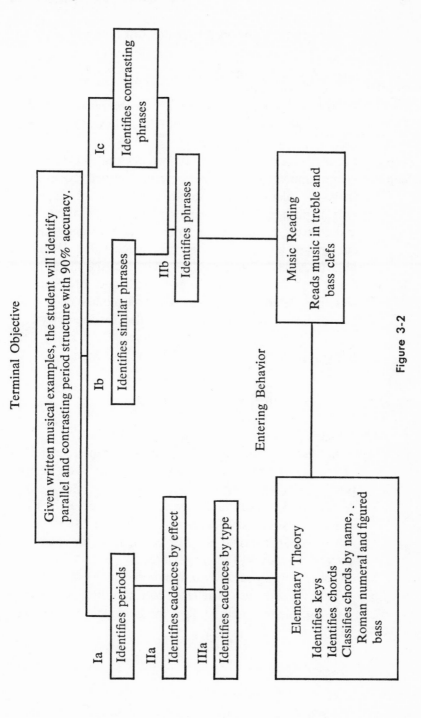

Figure 3-2

Steps Involved in Objective Analysis

Step 1   Identify terminal objective.

Step 2   Identify learner entry level.

Step 3   Starting at the terminal objective, ask the question, "What kind of capability would an individual have to possess to accomplish this objective?"

Step 4   Repeat procedure for each competency that is determined.

Step 5   As prerequisite competencies are determined, begin to arrange in hierarchical fashion. [To organize objectives type or print each component on a three-by-five-inch card and sort these cards on a large table. You may find the chalkboard too inflexible to be of much value. When the objectives have been arranged, they may be diagramed.]

Step 6   Continually check efforts to assess relevance of competencies thus determined and to weed out competencies that are inappropriately stated, too detailed for the entry level of the learner, etc. Ask the question, "Do I really need this competency?". . .

Self-Check Mastery Test

1.   What is the purpose or function of the pretest?

2.   What are the four categories of musical objectives for assessment? Briefly describe each one. (See "Exit Test for the Program.")

3.   What are appropriate categories for the objectives that you use in your music classes? (See the exit test.)

4.   What are appropriate modes of evaluation for each category of objectives? (See the exit test.)

5.   What is the purpose or function of the entry test?

6.   What is a sequence that leads to a terminal objective in a course that you teach? (See the guidelines for sequencing.)

4

selecting procedures
to achieve your objectives

Objectives

Upon mastering the content of this chapter, the reader should be able to:

1. Define "teaching method."
2. List traditional methods of teaching.
3. List the steps in the basic teaching strategy for cognitive objectives.
4. List several ways to individualize instruction.
5. List steps for a teaching strategy for psychomotor objectives.
6. List steps for a teaching strategy for affective objectives.

The theme developed throughout the preceding pages has emphasized student learning as the measure of an accountable music education program. Now we are ready to concentrate upon what a teacher does with reference to the total learning system. In the accountability model, instruction is not evaluated by some set of standards reflecting specific teaching methods or techniques. This often occurs in situations where supervisors or evaluators want their pet procedures used exclusively. Instead, the teacher is evaluated upon his ability to facilitate learning. He must be able to set up the learning conditions that lead to the attainment of stated objectives. W. James Popham has described the instructional strategy as "criterion-referenced instruction."

> This approach to instruction focuses primarily on the degree to which the learner can perform specified criterion behaviors. . . . a primary feature of criterion-referenced instruction is a preoccupation with the results of instruction, not the procedures used to promote them. It reflects an ends-oriented approach to instruction rather than a means-oriented approach. Since most educators concur that the ultimate index of an educational program's worth is the degree to which it benefits the learner, the increased support of criterion-referenced instructional approaches is gratifying.[1]

This position in no way degrades the process of teaching or demeans the teacher: quite the reverse is true. The teacher is freed to be as creative and innovative as possible in order to expedite student learning. However, his teaching procedures are more exposed and accountable. They must be efficient and effective.

The teacher, then, must structure the classroom environment to evoke student responses that lead to objectives (learning). The classroom environment is the "stimulus situation" that comprises the physical setting for student interaction. It consists of the music, materials, musical instruments, A-V equipment, teacher's demonstrations, small group discussions—everything presented for the pur-

---

[1] W. James Popham, "Objectives and Instruction" (paper presented at the American Educational Research Association Meeting, Los Angeles, Calif., February 1969). Used by permission.

pose of learning. Ideally, you organize and set up the conditions that elicit the "doing," and then get out of the way of student learning.

Traditional Teaching Methods

What is the actual behavior that a teacher uses to "teach" the student to behave in a way that he has never behaved before? What does a teacher do to induce him to interact with the environment to cause him to learn? The paradox is that we know of no teacher behavior that is always a causative agent. There is no best method. This truth is the very strength of behavioral objectives and their emphasis upon student performance. The only thing we really know about teaching is that the teacher attempts to structure appropriate stimulus situations which he hopes will elicit the students' responses that he has named as objectives. By using the consequences as reinforcing or modifying feedback he shapes students' behavior as specified in the objectives.

This discussion probably sounds quite theoretical. Yet even if we have our behavioral objectives, how many of us have taken time to thoroughly analyze what we are doing when we "teach," much less to try to delineate and consider alternative methods of achieving our stated goals? Systematic instruction depends upon alternatives to accommodate various learning styles, learning rates and interests of students. It is unwise to limit yourself to one method, and futile to search for one "best" method because of individual differences of students and differing requirements of objectives.

The experienced teacher will use one or another of the approaches, shifting to the most appropriate procedure for the specific task to be learned. Perhaps he may utilize several modes within a single lesson. Often he may adjust intuitively to the demands of the situation. The following section will summarize the "expository" and "interaction " methods with reference to the systematic instructional accountability model.

Expository Procedures

Exposition refers to teaching methods in which the teacher presents information, principles, problem solutions, examples, or other subject content to students. The content is usually presented in its final "predigested" form. The teacher assumes the dominant role. The activity of students can be covert (thinking), overt (taking notes, responding to questions, demonstrating the principles) or inert (sleeping). To get students involved the teacher should work for active participation and provide continuous feedback. In any music class musical performance provides a natural way of doing something with the information and material presented. Expository procedures include deduction, lecture, and demonstration.

Deduction. Deductive method is often used synonymously with expository method. In the deductive method students are given a generalization, principle or rule from which they are asked to deduce specific examples. Most often several sample examples and illustrations are provided by the instructor in the initial presentation. For instance, a rule for constructing major triads is presented. Several examples of major triads are provided by the instructor and the students are requested to generate several more. Research has shown that teaching with rules is superior to teaching without rules when speed of learning and retention were used as criteria.[2]

Lecture. The lecture is the most used and abused technique at the higher levels of schooling. The formal lecture is a highly structured verbal presentation. It is very efficient for dispensing verbal information such as facts, terms and principles to a large class. Although informing, telling and explaining have their places, the lecture by itself is not an acceptable method for systematic instruction. It is a one-way communication from teacher to student. The student has little opportunity for interaction or response. Some student response can be facilitated by providing outlines, guides, summaries, worksheets or study questions. A discussion and question period can be included at the end of the teacher talk. Seminars, dis-

---

[2] John T. Guthrie, "Expository Instruction Versus a Discovery Method," in *Current Research on Instruction,* Richard C. Anderson, et al., eds. (Englewood Cliffs, N.J.: Prentice-Hall, Inc., 1969), p. 265.

cussion groups and laboratory groups are utilized in many schools for this purpose. The lecture is a good method for organizing subject content but a poor method for achieving behavioral objectives.

Demonstration. Demonstrating is an effective and widely used technique in teaching musical knowledge and skill. You present a picture, an illustration, a model, a written or verbal example, or a nonverbal demonstration. You either show something or show how to do something: "Here it is—Look! Listen!" or "This is the way you do it: First. . .then. . ."

Much of music teaching, especially in performance groups, group lessons and individual lessons, consists of a *do this* command strategy. Teachers demonstrate and otherwise indicate *what they want.* This highly prescriptive approach should be directed toward stated objectives which students understand and accept. Each student must be allowed trial performances and provided with feedback to shape performance to achieve results (objectives).

Concrete examples (referents) and models (mockups) are especially important in early learning. Displays as bulletin boards and posters, and A-V presentations as slides and overhead transparencies can be used effectively. More is said about this in the next chapter.

Interaction Procedures

Interaction methods seek to eliminate many problems inherent in expository methods, especially the criticism of the teacher-centered, passive-learner, lock-step format. Even in large group situations, the student must respond if he is to learn. Interaction methods are intended to bring each learner into the learning situation as an active participant. The extent to which the individual student participates (responds) and actually achieves objectives is the measure of the effectiveness of the procedure. In many interaction procedures the learner is expected to assume a large measure of control over his learning objectives, materials, sequencing and evaluation. Interaction procedures include discussion, discovery and inquiry.

Discussion. The most obvious alternative to the lecture is the discussion. The one-way communication from teacher to pupil is extended to include pupil-to-teacher and pupil-to-pupil communication. Discussion can be very student centered unless dominated by the teacher. Old-fashioned recitation is a good example of the latter. It is a highly structured and often rote procedure for learning objectives. The other extreme is best illustrated by the encounter group where students freely exchange ideas, viewpoints, opinions and feelings without much regard for any prescribed instructional objectives. This is a particularly useful method for dealing with affective learnings; e.g., musical preferences and value judgments. The teacher's role is simply to restate and help clarify the ideas of the student.

It would seem that a middle approach between the two extremes would be most appropriate. The skilled teacher can direct discussion toward the stated learning objectives. As a moderator he can hold students reasonably on the track without dominating the discussion or simply dispensing verbal information. Care must be taken that discussions are not taken over by a few verbally adept students. This creates a lecture-type situation with an added liability. If students do not have some background in the content area and specific subject matter to be discussed, the session soon degenerates into a mutual exchange of ignorance, or perhaps a very quiet period.

Discovery. The "discovery method" presently enjoys popularity, a large educational following, and an ever-expanding mystique largely unsupported by research findings. Discovery method must be defined operationally if it is to be used in music teaching. There is much confusion regarding the usage of the terms "discovery," "problem solving," and "inquiry" as methods, especially since all three can be "guided" or "unguided."

As a rule of thumb, discovery method can be equated to the inductive method. In the inductive approach students move from specific observations to a generalization. Learners are provided with specific examples for which they find and state the rules. In the discovery method there are "correct" answers to be found. In contrast, problem solving refers to a higher level of induction which is more open ended. There may be no correct answer or perhaps many "correct" answers. Composing music is a problem-solving endeavor. There is ample room for risk-taking or experimentation here if the teacher will allow for it. There can certainly be no one correct answer as in a typical theory exercise. Problem solving also allows for the student to take more responsibility for his own learning. One elementary music teacher I know sends students to an adjoining room with rhythm instruments of their choice to "compose" a piece according to given parameters and then perform it for the class. The day I observed, the students composed and performed an ABA form with a *crescendo* in the "B" section. This is a good approach to individualized learning and creative problem solving.

Discovery method is not only a way to achieve objectives but also a good way to learn the scientific method. Although time consuming, this approach is useful in teaching students to collect data, formulate hypotheses (the tentative answers) and test answers. The way something is done—the process—can be prescribed in the curriculum. Process objectives are often written to assure this type of learning opportunity.

The teacher's role in the discovery method is that of a guide and facilitator of learning. He or she presents concrete examples and illustrations and lets students discover the concepts and principles. The teacher helps in this process by raising pertinent questions and /or providing answers to student questions (as in the inquiry method). Students find and state answers to achieve objectives. Thus we see that the discovery method can be placed on a continuum from the expository approach, where all information, concepts, principles and solutions are provided by the teacher, to "unguided discovery," where the student must locate all data, formulate and use concepts and principles, and find solutions for himself. Learning is most efficient when the teacher provides some guidance. For example, less time is wasted if the teacher presents or reviews the relevant concepts and principles that the student must use to solve the problem.

Inquiry. The inquiry method is closely related to discovery. Inquiry is used to teach the scientific method. The rationale suggests that the most important first step in any solution is knowing what questions to ask. Inquiry is a search strategy. Students attempt to zero in on the answer by asking questions proceeding from the general (Is it mineral?) to the specific (Is it a cymbal?). It resembles the old game of "Twenty Questions." The primary role of the teacher is to provide answers, usually limited to a simple yes or no, until the solution is achieved. The teacher may further modify the answer for guidance and cues, provide reinforcement, summarize, reword, review and call upon students in rotation.

Initially the teacher must structure the situation with an appropriate stimulus such as a picture, illustration, demonstration or verbal description. The students must also be informed of the rules of inquiry. For example, questions are asked and answered one at a time; a student can continue questioning until he has exhausted his line of reasoning; students can confer together; etc.

Inquiry in the above sense is student centered. The questions are student generated and student controlled. "Questioning" as a traditional method is usually teacher generated and controlled. The Socratic dialogue is the best example. Questions are directed to emphasize the inconsistencies and incorrect notions in the student's ideas. Posing or raising questions is a good technique for initiating and maintaining student activity toward stated objectives. The objectives themselves can be reworded into the interrogative mode. Norris M. Sanders' book *Classroom Questions, What Kinds?*[3] provides a handy source of questions derived from the Bloom taxonomy of the cognitive domain. You can adapt these questions for your musical objectives.

Simulations, role playing and game strategies. The idea behind these collective methodologies is to involve students, as much as possible, in practical, lifelike situations. The driver training simulator used in many driver education courses is a good example. Role-playing activities are advocated by many to help students understand the feelings of other people in various positions. The "teacher role" of the student tutor, discussed later in this chapter, provides a good illustration.

Team games are very effective to achieve a variety of musical objectives that involve drill and practice. When an elementary music objective relates to reading and playing rhythm patterns, use a game to create and sustain interest. First divide the class into two teams. Use appropriate rhythms that have been notated on large

---

[3]   (New York: Harper & Row Publishers, 1966).

display boards or on the chalkboard. A student plays one of the rhythm patterns and calls upon a member of his team to identify it. Teams alternate until each pupil has had an opportunity to play and respond at least once. A point is awarded for each correct answer. The game is fast moving and self-perpetuating. All students pay attention and listen to questions and answers. An incorrect answer can be corrected by the other team for a point. If answers are called out by others, the team loses a point. The game covers many students in a short time. The teacher can sit back, take notes, pinpoint problems, evaluate students and even check off objectives as they are achieved. A similar game can be played with tonal patterns. In this version the student plays the pattern on a xylophone or bells. His responding team member must sing it (perhaps with syllables) as he identifies it.

Use games to teach music listening objectives; e.g., to identify instruments, styles, or forms. Teams listen silently and then confer together to decide upon the answer. This usually stimulates lively discussions or heated debates. Teach instruments by sight, using pictures in a similar game. "Musical Lotto" is a commercially available game for this purpose. Students can make up riddles that identify the critical properties of musical instruments. Let them decide upon the three or four best clues. They can use books, pictures and other resources. Here are some examples: "I am made of brass; I have a circular shape; I was originally used by hunters. What am I?" "I have four strings; I must be played standing up; I have sloped shoulders. What am I?"

Students can scramble words, work crossword puzzles, use flashcards and use the spell-down technique to learn musical terms, symbols and signs. Let students generate examples as much as possible. Game making as well as game playing are good ways to individualize instruction. The possibilities seem limitless. But do not overuse the game strategy. It may degenerate into a time-killing technique.

A Teaching/Learning Strategy

Teaching strategy, in current educational terminology, refers to the teacher's approach for achieving stated objectives. Any of the preceding methods can be utilized as appropriate. Often the well-formulated objective itself will suggest the most efficient and effective means (activities in which to engage students) to attain it. The following strategy is presented as a model for most cognitive objectives. Obviously, any strategy will have to be adjusted to the specific objective and the learner. The tactics that comprise the basic teaching strategy are: 1) present and clarify objectives, 2) secure and maintain commitment to objectives, 3) review needed prerequisite learning, 4) provide situations and activities that lead to objectives, and 5) provide feedback.

Present and Clarify Objectives

Do not underestimate the importance of presenting and clarifying objectives. Studies indicate that learning is more efficient when the teacher communicates to students exactly what they are expected to do to demonstrate learning at the end of the instructional sequence. If we really knew how to teach anyone anything *directly* there would be no need to reveal objectives. However, since students must respond and interact with the learning environment they must have some idea of the intent of this interaction. If students do not find the relationship between the activity in which they are engaged and the objectives, learning may be minimal. Music students sing in chorus, play in band, study, drill, write exercises, take notes, outline material, watch a demonstration, review, listen to music, listen to lectures, take part in a discussion, etc., etc. This is all part of the interaction. But what specifically is the purpose of the activity and what are they to do with all of the information presented to them in order to demonstrate that they have learned it? This is precisely stated in your behavioral objectives. Students know what is expected of them: they have the needed guidance, can assume a greater degree of responsibility for their own learning, and can evaluate their own progress toward the attainment of objectives.

The following list illustrates several ways of revealing objectives.

1.   Tell students what they are expected to accomplish by the end of the unit (or course). Do not present a con-

fusing array of objectives. Deal them out as needed to guide and direct learning activities.

2. Give them a written copy of your objectives. Refer to the list often and suggest they use it for guidance. Let them know they *are* achieving the objectives on that list as they progress through various stages of the instructional sequence.

3. Use vocabulary that the student can easily grasp. For example, a behavioral objective may state: "Given recorded aural examples of music in which a different solo instrument is predominant, the student will identify each solo instrument by sound with at least 85 percent accuracy." The student objective could be stated: "Be able to identify the solo instrument in each recording you hear."

4. Give students examples of the expected terminal performance. Use demonstrations, illustrations, samples, pictures or models.

5. Present objectives prior to the learning task to assure direction and guidance. Of course, some affective objectives involving preferences and attitudes should not be revealed until later, if at all. It is inappropriate to inform the learner when trying to secure a nonreactive measure. He can fake it.

6. Question the group at appropriate intervals to determine if they recall and understand the objectives.

7. Review or summarize objectives as needed. Pupils may forget the purpose of the activities in which they are involved. Not much learning can occur under these circumstances.

8. Clarify each part of an objective so students understand the conditions under which they are to perform, the exact behavior they are to perform, the concepts involved and the acceptable standard of performance.

9. Use sample test questions to clarify the behavior.

10. Help students clarify their own objectives that they derive from a complex terminal task. Sequencing of learning is an individual affair which can perhaps best be

facilitated by assisting students to determine their own enabling objectives, materials and evaluative procedures.

Secure and Maintain Commitment to Objectives

Students must accept your objectives and be willing to undertake the learning tasks leading to their attainment. Without commitment there is no response; without response there can be no learning.

In Chapter 2, it was suggested that a rationale be included with each objective to assist learners in perceiving value. A discussion of the objective itself can help set the stage. Tell students about the benefits; encourage them to express possible benefits they perceive; show them what is in it for them. Relevance is the cry of the times. Set up expectations and create interest.

It helps to be inventive when "selling" your objectives. Use novel, unexpected and even shock techniques with demonstrations, visuals and mockups. This does not mean being phony or trite. Believing in what you stand for and what you are trying to accomplish can influence students to attain the prescribed objectives.

This discussion implies that students can either accept or reject your objectives, that alternative objectives are available, and students can choose what they want to learn. When students participate in setting objectives, they are more likely to accept them. Many teachers use a "contract" signed by student and teacher for this purpose. The contract format should include a statement of objectives (task description), materials needed, and procedures to be followed. The project can be jointly evaluated when it is presented to the class or to the teacher.

Maintaining commitment to objectives is largely a matter of success and reinforcement through feedback. Shifting mode of instruction and teaching materials (media) can help sustain interest. Review objectives and rationale when appropriate to focus upon the tasks.

Review Needed Prerequisite Learning

Entry tests determine if the student is adequately prepared to tackle the proposed learning tasks. Perhaps he must start at a lower level of objectives if he lacks background learning. Remedial work with the entire class may be necessary before instruction can begin. If only a few students lack the prerequisite competencies, they can be helped with individual tutoring, programed instruction or reference readings.

Assuming that students are ready to undertake the new learning tasks, a careful review of needed information, concepts, principles and/or skills should help facilitate the acquisition of objectives. Students must recall and use relevant knowledge and skills in the learning situation. When teaching toward the terminal objective "to identify period structure," the student may have to be reminded that phrases are located by marking cadences, and that cadences have different effects. A review of cadence types and their complete and incomplete effects may be necessary. Students may further be reminded that phrases can be similar (parallel) or different (contrasting). A review of this type helps establish learning set by focusing attention upon relevant stimuli. It also provides cues or prompts to give further direction to learning.

Provide Situations and Activities That Lead to Objectives

Once the learner knows the objectives and is committed to them, he must practice the behaviors called for in the objectives or at least engage in learning tasks that lead to the objectives. You can adapt the basic teaching methods discussed earlier to help the student attain your stated outcomes. First use expository methods to communicate the needed information and directions to initiate learning; then interaction methods to facilitate response. Set up the learning environment: assemble media; group students for large-group, small-group or individualized instruction. (See Figure 4-1.) The learner must practice the behaviors to be learned. Although a student may respond covertly (mentally), overt practice is an ob-

servable indicator of student progress toward objectives. He can
sing, play, write, speak, and generally do the things necessary to
reach objectives.

STRUCTURING THE LEARNING ENVIRONMENT FOR INTERACTION

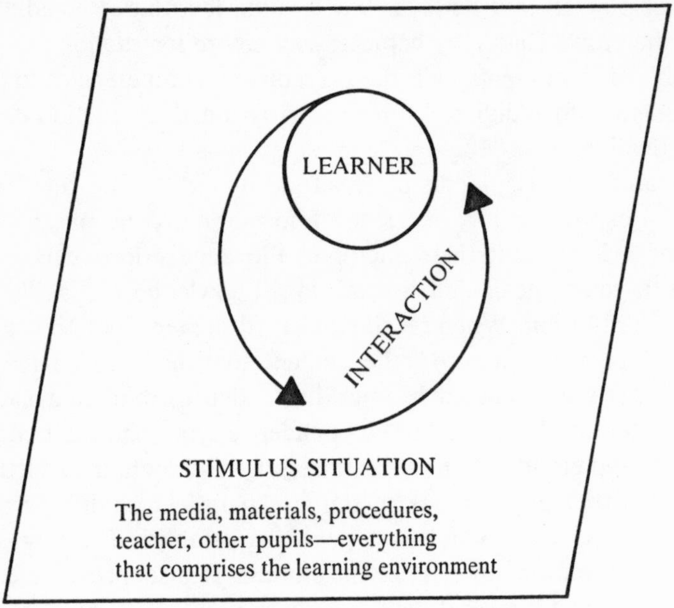

Figure 4-1

Asahel Woodruff has described this operation as setting the
"stage" for learning. The teacher should stand in the wings to direct, guide and coach. But he must let the student perform. In other
words the teacher must get out of the way of learning by allowing
the student to actively engage in learning activities.

This is probably of little concern to most music teachers. We
have had students *doing* for years—singing, creating, improvising,
composing, listening, and moving. The student must practice the
behaviors specified in the objectives by interacting with teachers,
students, and/or instructional media. It seems so obvious, but too
often students (and teachers) do not relate activity to outcomes and
means to ends. In an "activity curriculum" learners are so busy
doing that they are often not aware of what they are supposed to

be *learning*. Whatever activities we provide for pupils should lead to our stated objectives.

The problem with so many procedures, techniques, methods of teaching, music lessons, method books, and other published materials and texts is that they are not directed toward any specified objectives of instruction. Without objectives they remain just something to do. Instead of blindly following a method book lesson by lesson, select activities supported by whatever materials and media are appropriate that lead to your stated objectives. This is what students should practice. Here you find the drills and exercises that lead to learning.

Provide Feedback

Now that students are involved in doing to achieve objectives they must be informed about how well they are doing for learning to be efficient.

Programed instructional materials provide the best examples of feedback for this strategy. They indicate immediately the correctness or appropriateness of each response. A good teacher can also provide the correct answer or confirmation although not as efficiently as a program. He can do this informally by questioning, observing performance, relating the adequacy of performance, and encouraging self-evaluation. The student makes a response and the teacher reinforces it if it is correct by saying "Good," "Yes that's right," etc., or indicates verbally or by gesture if it is wrong. Ignoring a response will facilitate its extinction.

Bloom and others have advocated the use of "formative" evaluation in usual group-based instruction using feedback/correction procedures.[4] Formative evaluation is designed as an integral part of the teaching/learning process. This is contrasted to "summative" evaluation which is used as an end-of-course or terminal assessment. Standardized tests and teacher-made tests are both appropriate for summative evaluation and grading.

---

[4] Benjamin S. Bloom, et al., *Formative and Summative Evaluation of Student Learning* (New York: McGraw-Hill, 1971).

Formative tests are incorporated into the teaching/learning process to diagnose learning difficulties (or reinforce learning) and to prescribe alternate instructional material and procedures to achieve objectives. Like a conductor in rehearsal they detect and suggest corrections for errors in performance. They not only show what students have not learned but they provide feedback for the teacher about what aspects of instruction need modification for improvement. Formative tests should occur at frequent intervals to identify unmastered material before final grading. The tests themselves should not be used for grading. If they are incorporated in the grading system, they might lose their diagnostic function in assessing ongoing learning progress. They can be graded "pass" (mastery) or "more work needed" or "not yet." This allows for the feedback and guidance function to operate in the learning process. Obviously the tests must be short so that they do not take up an inordinate amount of instructional time.

Formative evaluation should also be built into teaching materials and media. Programed instructional materials illustrate this important function best. Programed instruction usually provides entrance and exit tests for each learning unit, in addition to the immediate confirmation of every student response. You can incorporate formative evaluation effectively in other more traditional teaching materials. Use flashcards with answers written on the back for easy self-check. Develop self-scoring tests to accompany texts, lessons, method books and other instructional media. Fold up and staple the answer sheets to the tests. Include page numbers with the answers for easy reference, confirmation and review. With this approach, each student can check his answers at the precise time he is ready to do so—at school or at home. Feedback should be immediate for most efficient learning. Students can also exchange papers or grade their own within the class period.

Multiple-choice questions are easiest to grade quickly but other types of questions can be used. Look again at the Exit Test for the Program in Chapter 3, and the Self-Check Mastery Tests at the end of the chapters. Some cognitive objectives have no "correct" answers, so they cannot be measured by objective tests. Motor skill objectives and affective objectives present similar measurement problems. These objectives require guidelines, rating scales, check sheets or informal observations to monitor student progress toward their attainment. Chapter 6 further investigates test construction.

Individualized Instruction

The emphasis upon mastery learning for each student requires individualized instruction. However, individualized instruction does not necessarily refer to "one student studying by himself all of the time" as some critics have suggested. Individualization can occur in a group setting. It essentially means that alternative materials, procedures and objectives are provided for the student. It is the essence of a continuous progress program. As much as possible the learner can learn at his own best rate of speed, evaluate his own achievement, and select his own best learning style, sequence, and what he wants to learn.

> One of the major observations in the current period is that the key to learning is individualization— the patterning of learning to suit the individual, his idiom, his style, his way of learning. In essence, an ultimate objective might be for every child to have his own teacher, and perhaps one way of achieving this is to have each pupil play the teacher role. As a tutor, he learns through teaching, and he also learns as a recipient, as a tutee when he is being taught.[5]

Considerable evidence has been collected to support the hypothesis that students can teach other students effectively. Rather than emphasizing academic competition, this approach encourages students to help each other to learn. I know of one school system that utilizes high school instrumentalists as private teachers for elementary pupils. The "teachers" are closely monitored by the band director and paid according to experience. In my own teaching, I have often asked a student who was having a learning problem and was further confused by my "comprehensive explanations" to seek assistance from another student who was not having similar difficulties. Learning has always been remarkable.

---

[5] Alan Gartner, et al., *Children Teach Children* (New York: Harper and Row, Publishers, 1971), p. 8.

Research has further revealed a rather surprising result—on the basis of achievement tests, the tutor learns much more than the tutee. The student tutor must organize the material for presentation and in so doing manage his own learning. In the teacher role he acquires new attitudes toward school, teaching, teachers and learning. He literally learns how to learn.[6]

Attempt to individualize as much as possible within the constraints of time, facilities, equipment and personnel. Read the small but penetrating book *Individualized Instruction, A Descriptive Analysis* by Maurice Gibbons for many suggestions.[7] It will suffice here to list some ways that you can move toward individualizing your music program.

1. Provide alternative objectives
2. Provide alternative activities
3. Provide alternative materials and media
4. Assess entering behavior (needs assessment)
5. Allow students to move on to other learning on the basis of pretest competency
6. Provide for individual pacing
7. Provide remedial help
8. Provide tutorial help (use paraprofessionals, volunteers, parents and/or student tutors)
9. Provide for independent study
10. Provide programed instructional material
11. Allow for self-evaluation
12. Provide feedback (formative evaluation)

Teaching Motor Skills

Much of the preceding discussion has been directed toward cognitive learning. However, most music programs emphasize the acquisition of techniques and skills. The dichotomy is quickly resolved if skills are related to the *application* of important concepts and principles. Students can learn more efficiently if all objectives

---

6   Gartner, *Children Teach Children*, pp. 1-7.

7   (New York: Teachers College Press, 1971).

have been clarified; learners then understand why they are doing what they are doing.

The demonstration method is most efficient for teaching skills. The process is sometimes called model learning. It consists of recurring cycles of three major steps: 1) demonstration, 2) practice and 3) evaluation.

First the teacher presents the skill that the student is to acquire. He clarifies this performance objective through actual demonstration, oral instructions, written directions and/or illustrations as charts, diagrams or pictures. Next he provides the learner with opportunities to practice the skill. The teacher "shapes" the learner's behavior by first accepting gross approximations and then requiring gradually more refined performance until the terminal performance is met. This does not mean that the learner should practice mistakes. His attempts are guided by the goal (model performance). He must be encouraged to evaluate himself and modify as he practices. He should be directed to drill upon specific movement problems to correct them.

Studies have shown that practice is most efficient when spaced. The learner should be encouraged to utilize short but frequent practice periods alternated with short rest periods. The student can take another hint from research and from professional musicians. That is, he should practice silently, actually fingering instruments and/or thinking through the music while waiting his turn to perform. This is another type of individualization that can be easily promoted in a group situation.

When learners are having difficulties with certain movements direct physical guidance and "fading" techniques[8] can be used effectively. For example, the string teacher may physically bow with a beginning student, gradually releasing his grip on the bow until the child is bowing in the desired manner by himself. Even at higher academic levels the conducting instructor may physically hold the baton with the neophyte to lead him through difficult conducting problems as *fermati*. (A video tape recorder can also be used to great advantage for feedback.)

---

[8] In the fading technique, the stimulus is gradually changed so that finer discriminations are required after several correct discriminations of a grosser nature have been successfully made.

Physical guidance and learning from a model demonstration depend upon establishing kinesthetic stimuli within the learner which will maintain the appropriate behavior after the guiding external stimulus has been removed. There remain only the external stimuli which elicit the response, in this case musical notation. These internal states are quite accessible to learners in terms of bodily consciousness or proprioceptive feedback. "Proprioceptive" refers to stimuli produced within an organism by movement of its own tissues; e.g., muscle feel. This feel is manifest in much musical behavior as singing or playing an instrument while reading music. Proprioceptive stimuli mediate rhythmic/metric timing and motor skills for performance. They are closely allied with the affective performance behavior discussed in the next section.

Finally, in model learning we ask the student to imitate in order to acquire skills. Imitation is a human phenomenon and probably the primary stimulus for all of learning. The student imitated his parents while learning to speak and was reinforced for appropriate discriminations. He imitates his peers and sometimes his teachers. Remember that imitation is a phenomenon that we do not know how to generate predictably, but which happens nevertheless. In the end we merely take advantage of the learner's imitative behavior. We know that imitation will probably take place and we attempt to provide appropriate models of behavior. Again note that we are not "teaching" in the sense of imparting. We are arranging stimuli and manipulating the student's environment, hoping that his innate, interactive devices will cause him to respond in accordance with our objectives.

Teaching Toward Affective Objectives

Affective learnings include such outcomes as attitudes, preferences, values and aesthetic sensitivity. Since affective outcomes do not exist in isolation from cognitive and psychomotor learnings, many authorities argue against creating separate, artificial domains. They point out that affective learning is an inevitable by-product of other learnings and learning situations. Students not only learn a subject content or a skill, but in the process they learn to like or dislike it. There is an interaction of thinking, doing and feeling. Cognitive and motor-skill objectives equip the student to perform. He *can do*. Affective learnings will determine if under appropriate conditions he *will do*.

As with cognitive learning we infer attitudes from the behavior of the learner. Attitudes are positive or negative predispositions of varying intensity toward music or musical situations and can be described in terms of approach or avoidance behavior tendencies. Does the student pursue or avoid the learning? Mager proposes that positive attitudes toward a subject can be influenced through positive, pleasant experiences and modeling of appropriate behavior.[9] Gross teacher behaviors to foster positive attitudes would be: 1) clarifying objectives and presenting rationale, 2) creating expectations and securing success, and 3) providing positive reinforcement and maintaining feedback. The manner of teaching seems more important than what is to be taught. Students must want music. Promote that interest and want.

Shaping musical preferences is a closely related problem. A music teacher cannot tell his students what to like. However, he is a musical leader in the community and provides such a model. If he is respected, admired and emulated, he can have considerable influence.

The aesthetic dimension of affective behavior requires investigation also. How is it facilitated? Certainly the aesthetic, emotional, feelingful or expressive aspects of musical performance can be approached through proprioceptive response. A common-sense expression long used in skill learning is "try to get the feel of it." We work in many ways as teachers trying to guide and help students get the feel.

The performer is often instructed to play with "feeling." Similarily, the conductor is expected to conduct expressively and "feelingfully"—not mechanically. This does not mean that he should project personal feelings into music or immerse himself, so to speak, in a sea of sensuousness and emotion. Rather, the response is feelingful in the sense of motion or kinesthesis—not emotion as it is

---

[9] Robert F. Mager, *Developing Attitude Toward Learning* (Palo Alto, Calif.: Fearon Publishers, 1968).

usually connoted. The feeling is perceived in the music itself or, more specifically, in the musical score as it is read. The performer further "feels with" the music as he performs it. He feels the tonal tendencies, phrase movement, melodic rise fall, unexpected turns of phrase, rhythmic drives, stresses and inhibitions, and harmonic movement to repose at cadences. They are felt as muscular and visceral tensions (proprioceptive stimuli), and yet are not really emotions.

This we can teach by systematically emphasizing the expressive structure of the music. In teaching aesthetic sensitivity the teacher may select an objective such as, "The student will respond to the phrasing and 'line' of music." The enabling objectives can be approached through the activities of performing, moving, listening and creating.

1. The student marks phrases in the music he is performing.
2. The student sings and/or plays phrases.
    a. moving the line to cadence
    b. building to climax and release
    c. using dynamic shading
    d. using rubato
3. The student indicates phrase feel by movement and by diagram.
4. The student selects the "best" performance of a phrase and writes reasons for his choices (preferences).
5. The student improvises phrases.
6. The student composes phrases.

Self-Check Mastery Test

1. What is a 'teaching method?"
2. What are several traditional teaching methods?
3. What are the steps of the basic teaching strategy for cognitive objectives?
4. What are several ways that you can individualize instruction?
5. What are the steps to teach psychomotor objectives?
6. What are ways to teach toward affective objectives?

5

utilizing instructional media
to achieve your objectives

Objectives

Upon mastering the content of this chapter, the reader should be able to:

1. Define and give examples of instructional media.
2. List uses and advantages of the new media in teaching.
3. List general criteria for selecting media.
4. List levels of media.
5. Outline how to select media for each tactic within the basic teaching strategy.

"Media" is a provocative and permeating word in contemporary society. For most people it conjures up a monstrous image of modern mass communication comprised of television, telephone, radio, newspapers, satellites and laser beams. Some catchy, confusing phrases of Marshall McLuhan come to mind. To most music teachers, the media are closely associated with popular peer culture, as exemplified by pop records, picture magazines, movies, comic books, jargon and dress. "Instructional media," on the other hand, refer to the audio-visual aids used to enhance or jazz up a music lesson. The A-V aids are especially useful at those times when a teacher is not prepared: "What should I do today? . . .Hey, how about that great film on Buxtehude I ran across yesterday in the back of the closet!" Although the varied use of media (gimmicks and gadgets) can create enthusiasm and interest, their purpose is not simply to entertain. The primary use of any instructional media is the attainment of objectives. They are not just aids but integral components of the total instructional system.

Understanding Media

The first step in understanding media in education is to reduce the term to a basic definition. A medium is a way of conveying or effecting something. The preceding chapter investigated the procedures to be used for attaining objectives. The perceptive reader should have noticed that there could be no method without a means of effecting it. If students are to interact to learn, they must interact with something. If students are going to use information, that information must be communicated to them in some way.

Instructional media are ways of conveying instructional messages and effecting or facilitating learning. The spoken word and the textbook are common media for presenting and communicating instructional messages. However, the term is most often used in a more restricted sense to refer to the electronic and mechanical means of communication, the "new" media.

Media can record, store and reproduce an event, or even transport it through time and space. Media provide flexibility in presentation. An event can be speeded up, slowed down, stopped, reversed, resequenced and edited in many ways. It can be transmitted to millions of people simultaneously or perhaps to only a single learner.[1]

A distinction is made between the instructional materials and equipment in terms of software and hardware. In general, "software" refers to the subject-matter content that the student is to learn. "Hardware" refers to the machine, equipment, box or other device that stores and/or transmits the subject content.

The following listing is intended to illustrate the wide spectrum of traditional and new media available or potentially available to music teachers for communicating instructional messages. Hardware, software and techniques of presentation are interspersed.

"Natural" Media

Sound: vocal or instrumental demonstrations, as modeling rhythm or melody

Speech: directions, explanations, guest speakers, lectures

Gesture: conducting, signalling, facial expression

Real things: musical instruments, performing groups, conductors, performers, artifacts.

"Artificial" Media

Simulations: models, mockups, games, dramatizations, role playing.

Displays: posters, chalkboard, flip-chart with easel, feltboard, magnetic board, pegboard, exhibits.

Printed material: textbooks, reference books, paperback books, workbooks, worksheets, method books, etudes, sheet music, outlines, study guides, pamphlets, leaflets, newspapers, magazines, microfilm, microfiche, programed materials, programed books, teaching machines. (Local development of

---

[1] J. V. Edling and C. F. Paulson, "Understanding Instructional Media" in *The Contribution of Behavioral Science To Instructional Technology* (Monmouth, Oregon: Teaching Research Division, Oregon State System of Higher Education), p. IV-9.

printed materials is aided by many new printing and copy-
ing processes.)

Graphic representation: diagrams, drawings, sketches, charts,
graphs, cartoons, maps, globes.

Still pictures: photographs, paintings, 35 mm slides, filmstrips,
opaque projection, overhead projection.

Motion pictures: 16 mm, 8 mm, filmloops, cartridge loading,
single-concept films.

Television: educational television, video tape recording, EVR
(electronic video recording with playback unit), commercial television.

Audio: radio, telephone, tape recording (reel-to-reel, cassette),
disc recordings, synthesizers, electronic instruments, tuners,
metronomes.

Multimedia: sound motion pictures, talking books, sound
filmstrip, sound slide set, sound on slide, sound page
(studymaster), audio card systems, taped teaching demonstration with a workbook or method book using a cassette
playback unit, commercial or locally produced multimedia packages, computer-assisted instruction.

The Communication Problem

A revolution in communication and technology has been reshap-
ing the world in which we live. However, it has hardly touched the
mainstream of institutionalized education. By and large education
remains a Victorian, artisan operation in the midst of the knowledge
and communications explosion. School methods are generally out
of date and ineffectual for competing with the fast-paced communications devices and messages that bombard students during out-
of-school time.

Small wonder that children are discouraged at the prospect
of sitting at a desk for twelve years of rigidly sequenced education. Their preschool learning took place in a highly mediated, high information density, unstructured environment.
The school should add structure and direction to the learning
process, but not by decreasing the level of information avail-

able to children or by relying on print and speech as the only
media forms in regular use.[2]

As noted above, many new media are available but they are not
being utilized. Studies indicate that the verbal information/
memory pattern is still dominant in the classroom. Teachers dis-
pense information, make assignments from dated textbooks and
test—the old "lecture-textbook-recitation" method. In contrast to
this excessive verbalism and irrelevant material, the mass media
offer our students fast-moving television and radio programing
movies, pop records, picture magazines and comic books. All create
interference not easily surmounted by a slow, dull classroom pace.
Figure 5-1 illustrates the interference as "noise" entering the trans-
mission channel. Teachers are "tuned out" as students "cop out."
The new instructional media can help teachers compete.

Research studies have also provided evidence that people attend
selectively to the diverse stimuli in their environment. Perception
refers to the human capacity to gain meaning from the environment through the senses. To facilitate perception the organism must
filter and organize the millions of undifferentiated sense impressions
that constantly assault it. However, the process can become extremely limiting. Because the central nervous system is capable of
utilizing only a small portion of the sensory information received,
the human being can only attend to about seven different stimuli
(things) simultaneously. What a person consciously attends to or
what he unconsciously screens depends upon his psychological pre-
disposition or "set." This learning set is a result of his cultural environment, values, previous training, experience, present interests
and needs. The perceptual screening and selection process is also
rather ominous. What we are—what we have learned to be—determines to a large extent what we perceive and learn from our
environment. The trained musician will hear more music than a
nonmusician, and he will hear music more completely. Background
movie music is an example. Musicians are tuned in to music. Look

---

[2] John B. Haney and Eldon J. Ullmer, *Educational Media and the Teacher*
(Dubuque, Iowa: William C. Brown Company Publishers, 1970), p. 4. Used
by permission.

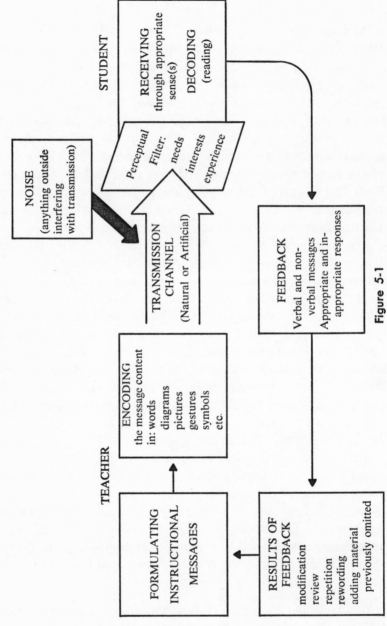

TEACHER-PUPIL COMMUNICATION FOR LEARNING

Figure 5-1

again at Figure 5-1. How can students be taught to perceive like musicians? A teacher can heighten awareness of the important stimuli and help students tune in music with the new media.

The teacher needs to consider as many appropriate devices as possible to overcome outside interferences and to penetrate the perceptual screen. He must effectively compete with the commercial, mass communications media. He can use different media in the repetitions needed for display, presentation, demonstration, practice and evaluation. Innovative programs have tried to shift modes of media, utilize varying methods and emphasize fast action to overcome boredom and create interest. The educational television program, *Sesame Street*, is perhaps the best known illustration of this approach. Media can help the teacher get through to students.

As we saw in the instructional model and again in Figure 5-1, communication is not a one-way channel. Telling does not result in learning. Effective communication is a two-way interaction. Channels can be varied: there can be communication flow between teacher and pupil, media and pupil, teacher with media and pupil, and pupil and pupil. See Figure 5-2.

The Teacher's Role in Selecting and Using Media

Perhaps the role of the teacher as a "classroom manager," "environment setter," or "organizer of stimuli" will become clearer now. Media are not isolated aids to instruction, or something added to instruction. In the systems approach media are integral components of the total system. They are literally the means of attaining objectives. Put another way, the teacher must select the media that will best facilitate learning. He arranges the "stuff" with which the learner will interact to achieve objectives.

Your job, then, is to assemble all materials, musical equipment and A-V hardware needed for student interaction. Choices must be made. The primary consideration, of course, is the objectives to be attained. Generally, objectives and learning tasks will suggest a medium that is appropriate. It is likely that several media will be suitable, providing alternative means. This helps provide for varying student interests and learning styles.

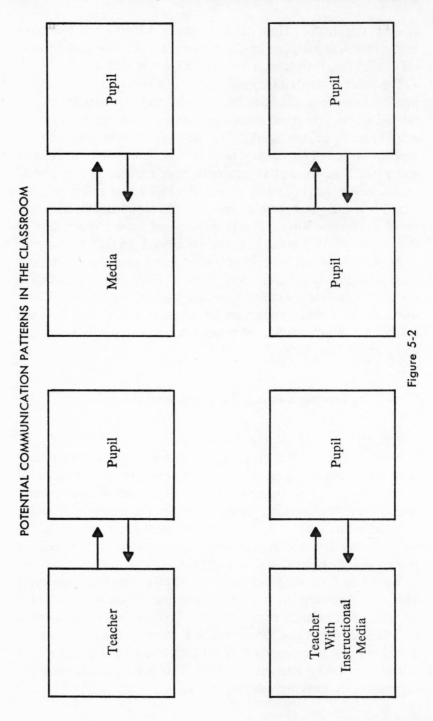

POTENTIAL COMMUNICATION PATTERNS IN THE CLASSROOM

Figure 5-2

Final selection will depend upon such criteria as quality and fidelity, level of difficulty, availability, and cost. Music teachers need good aural examples and models. Poor fidelity of sound, scratched recordings and out-of-date movies do not provide fitting communication for musical learning. Equipment must be of the highest quality possible for best simulation. Furthermore, the media may be designed for a specific student achievement level. Some may be too sophisticated or perhaps too simple for your purposes. To avoid this problem you must preview all materials. Availability brings many additional considerations. Is the material commercially available? Is it possible to prepare locally? How much time would be required for production? Is necessary hardware available when needed? Is it portable and easily handled? Finally, cost is an important constraint. Purchasing and production costs severely limit the widespread use of many media. One important advantage of listing alternative media (and if possible running research studies) is to determine comparative cost effectiveness. Often inexpensive means are more effective than costly ones. Consider the computer as an expensive page turner for some programmed material that can be presented as well in a scrambled book.

Recently I visited an elementary music room. The chairs were arranged in a large circle with a table in the center. On and under the table were Orff instruments, bells, and rhythm instruments of all types. The room also contained a piano, bulletin boards, chalkboards, books, music, posters, charts, record player, listening posts with earphones, tape recorder, overhead projector and several autoharps. Think of planning a lesson in a setting like this. How would you set up the specific stimulus situation for student interaction with the media, other students and/or you (the teacher) to achieve a particular objective?

Levels of Media

The rule-of-thumb notion that learning progresses from simple to complex, from concrete to abstract, from known to unknown, and from crudeness to precision provides yet another approach for selecting media for objectives. You can choose the alternatives that are most appropriate for the level and learning styles of the students. The results of research are inconclusive and sometimes conflicting, but evidence suggests that the three basic levels of media have their counterparts in learning styles and ability levels. The three basic levels of media are: 1) real things, 2) representations or simulations of real things, and 3) symbols for real things.

Direct Experience with Real Things

The most immediate and concrete teaching strategy is to present the actual "thing" being learned directly to one or more of the pupils' senses. Learning is rooted in firsthand experience. Most learning in early grades is accomplished this way. Little ones see, hear, touch and try. At this level, simple exposure to the stimulus object may not be enough. Actual contact with the object, especially manipulating it and noting consequences, will better facilitate learning.

Firsthand experience is also needed for older children, especially those of lower academic ability. Realistic materials will most effectively facilitate perception of the referent in concept learning.

Generally, the realistic situation that contains many irrelevant features is best for learning and transfer of learning because students must discriminate between the relevant and irrelevant details.[3]

The "doing" part of music education has always been involved with direct experience. Children are helped to develop a physical feel for beat, meter and rhythmic patterns. They are guided to feel the upward and downward motion of melody and the movement of the phrase to cadence.

Actual musical phenomena can be used at all levels. Musical instruments can be presented and demonstrated. It is a real experience to take a piano apart and explore it. Vocalists, instrumentalists, conductors and performing groups can be brought to the classroom.

---

[3] Robert M. W. Travers, *Man's Information System* (Scranton, Pa.: Chandler Publishing Company, 1970), pp. 135-39.

Real-life encounters can be structured through field trips. Students can visit rehearsals and performances of orchestras, bands, chamber groups, choirs and opera companies.

Perhaps this level of experiencing media is best exemplified by the Manhattenville Music Curriculum and the Contemporary Music Project. Both approaches to curricula are based upon real-life concerns. Regardless of ability level or experience, all students do what musicians do—sing, play an instrument, compose, analyze, conduct, and make value judgments about performances and musical worth. Neophyte musicians interact with the musical "stuff" that is needed for them to function as a practicing musician at their level of ability.

Simulating Real Experience

It is often impossible or impractical for a learner to engage in real-life experience. Problems of time, place, space and cost may make the desired environment inaccessible for educational purposes. Furthermore, it is extremely inefficient to try to learn everything by firsthand, concrete experience. School is a contrived learning environment—at worst, out of contact with reality; at best, simulating real-life experience in an effective, efficient way. Here teachers can use media to contrive learning experiences to simulate life. Marshall McLuhan describes media as "the extensions of man." Media allow us to extend beyond the limitations of the immediate, concrete environment in time and space. As television has shown, we can be taken anywhere for a vicarious experiencing of an actual happening: to the moon, to Oswald's murder, to an Asian war.

Several types of simulations are available for the music teacher. Each will be briefly discussed to bring out its unique advantages.

Concrete representation. Concrete representation refers to a model or mockup that replicates the original in detail. Visual representations can be scaled up or down. They are usually three dimensional to facilitate interaction. Since they can be handled, they approach real, firsthand experience. Teachers can use mockups of instruments with cutaway sections, models of the symphony orchestra, home-built instruments or even long coil springs to simulate vibrating strings that demonstrate vibration and overtones. Aural models provide another dimension. High-fidelity recordings bring us sounds that replicate original sources.

Pictorial representation. We get much information from pictorial or iconic representations of real-life experience. The old cliché "A picture is worth a thousand words" seems to fit. Some research has indicated that because of human perceptual limitations ". . .visuals closely representing line drawings and containing the essence of the information to be transmitted would be more effective and more efficient in facilitating learning than would be more detailed illustrations, which would have to be coded initially by the central nervous system before being transmitted."[4] The study concluded that the lines which border objects are stored in memory, and they can be more directly conveyed by line drawings. In iconic representations the features correspond directly to their real-life counterparts. They include motion pictures, flat or projected photographs, drawings, sketches, and paintings. Analogue representations, on the other hand, do not correspond to some bit of realia, but they are often as informative. They include diagrams, maps, charts, and graphs. A diagram of the form of a symphonic movement can be used quite effectively in a demonstration.

Interaction. Real-life experience can also be simulated through role playing, dramatizations and games. (See Chapter 4.)

Symbolizing Real Experience

A symbol represents a thing or event in the real world. Symbols include the written and spoken word, musical notation, and various abstract formulas. Symbolic representation is the most used, yet most abstract mode of presentation and communication. It is most appropriate for higher levels of learning, but certainly usable (if not overused) at all levels of instruction. The danger lies in the disassociation of symbol (concept) from the referent (actual ob-

---

[4] Francis M. Dwyer, Jr., "Adapting Visual Illustrations for Effective Learning," in *Current Research and Instruction*, Richard C. Anderson, et al., eds. (Englewood Cliffs, N.J.: Prentice-Hall, Inc., 1969), p. 258.

ject or event for which the symbol stands). Concepts must be rooted in concrete experience in order to facilitate meaningful verbal learning.

Common symbolic media include textbooks, workbooks, method books, study sheets, outlines and programed materials. Note that iconic representations are often used with symbolic representations —the pictures or illustrations that clarify the text.

Media and Instructional Strategies

The basic teaching/learning strategy presented in Chapter 4 requires the use of media. It can therefore provide a final set of considerations for selecting media. Each step of the strategy is reviewed here to incorporate appropriate media for its facilitation. The teacher's verbal directions and verbal presentations are the assumed baselines for the discussion.

Present and Clarify Objectives

A verbal or written presentation is the common method of revealing objectives. An overhead projector or slide display can be effectively incorporated, using diagrams, illustrations and important cues. Objectives should be stated using vocabulary at the student's level of comprehension.

Media can be used effectively to provide a model for terminal and enabling objectives. This is especially helpful for motor-skill and affective objectives. Live, videotaped, or filmed demonstrations can introduce the behavior. Audio recordings can present model musical performances. These provide the student with models of the behavior, conditions and level of competence expected of him.

Secure and Maintain Commitment to Objectives

Many of the media that are used to reveal and clarify objectives will concurrently help secure attention and initial commitment to objectives. Impressive demonstrations, attractive visuals, displays, exhibits and audio models will help generate enthusiasm. A guest performer or a field trip can be effective; films can stimulate interest in the topic or unit of study. A written or verbal rationale is often utilized to communicate the values to be derived from the objectives. This can be followed by a written contract to cement the commitment.

Shifting modes of media is the primary tactic for maintaining interest. Many sources are available to present content in a variety of ways. Try different channels of communication over the same content, or a multimedia approach. Like musical variation and development, the use of various media sustains interest and deepens meaning.

Assess Entering Behavior and Provide for Remedial Learning

Media can provide remedial and review material to bring deficient learners up to entry level. Reference books, outlines, study guides and verbal reminders are possible media to facilitate recall of important prerequisite competencies and concepts. Pictures, diagrams and illustrations may also be helpful. Programed texts and materials are probably the best examples of individualized instruction for acquiring needed entering behavior.

Provide Situations and Activities That Lead to Objectives

The teacher of the future will spend less time dispensing information and drilling skills, and more time managing media. The knowledge explosion, the communications revolution and the rise of technology portend this change.

> Thus a teacher is asking too much of himself to try personally to provide all stimuli required for learning. Let the media do it. The teacher's job is to organize the circumstances that provide the best opportunity for learning and to ensure that learning takes place. He can ease his own burden if he uses media to its best advantage and builds replicable instructional episodes around media forms that can be re-

peated for successive classes. In plain talk, once he has the "system working," he can spend less time talking and more time on planning and evaluation. He can cease being a drill sergeant and become instead an education executive.[5]

Use media to present or supply information. Instructional messages, subject content and managerial instructions can be displayed by overhead projection, still pictures, print, wall displays, illustrations, or multimedia sources.

Media can provide a stimulus for discussion, problem solving, musical composition or musical analysis. Movies, slide displays, film strips and audio recordings are suitable for these purposes.

Use media to provide a stimulus for applying information in practice and drill. The learner must be able to control the display for active participation. He must be able to control the pace and perhaps the sequence. He must be able to repeat portions as necessary. Programed materials, teaching machines, computer-assisted instruction, audio-tutorial methods, workbooks, worksheets and even the textbook provide for this type of interaction in varying degrees. The approach can be adapted to movies. Instead of running a film from beginning to end, stop at appropriate times to ask questions, provide cues, and generally direct learning toward the stated objectives.

Achieving aural-perception objectives. The use of a medium as a stimulus is best understood by considering a behavioral objective as a learning outcome or response. We must choose the type of medium that will elicit the response described in the objective. For example, consider the following objective. "Upon hearing appropriate musical examples, the learner will identify each as monophonic, homophonic or polyphonic with at least 75 percent accuracy." This objective can be achieved in one period by most fifth graders when media are employed. The following account summarizes the actions of one committee to achieve this objective.

The process was to work back from the outcome (objective) to the eliciting stimulus and then to choose specific media. (See Figure

[5] Haney and Ullmer, *Educational Media and the Teacher*, p. 7. Used by permission.

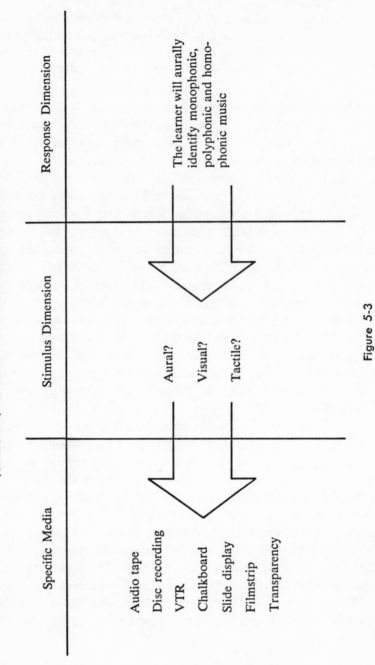

Figure 5-3

5-3.) The objective requires aural discrimination; thus, aural stimuli must be used. However, the visual channel can be effectively used also to graphically illustrate the meaning of the terms. (The tactile channel was considered inappropriate for this aural perception objective.)

Next, the specific media had to be selected. What would convey the sound? Disc recordings would be possible but it would be difficult to handle the many short examples. The examples were recorded on tape along with the verbal explanations.

Visuals were suggested to help students "see" what the music sounds like. Illustrations could be drawn on the chalkboard. Slides, transparencies or a filmstrip might be used. The overhead transparency was selected as the medium because it is easily seen by all students. It is colorful and permanent. It requires less time to produce than the filmstrip or slides and it costs less. The complete presentation could have been videotaped if a closed circuit television system was available. It was not.

The finished learning module consisted of twelve transparencies and a taped track with narration, examples, and suggestions for practice and assessment. Some of the visuals are presented in Figure 5-4.

Thus, to belabor the obvious, aural perception objectives are primarily approached through the auditory channel. Yet visual stimuli can play an auxiliary, clarifying role, along with the spoken word for explanation, direction and cues.

Achieving knowledge objectives. Knowledge level objectives can also be attained through a variety of media. At this stage of the teaching strategy, media are most effective for presentation and drill. For example, overhead transparencies with a permanent staff can be used for teaching notation. Overlays can consist of notes, clefs and scaled letter names. The letters stay in order but move as a block to accommodate the particular clef being demonstrated. This illustrates the principle of the alphabetic note relationship that never changes. (3M Company has several sets of transparency masters for music instruction.)

Games are appropriate to use to practice and drill knowledge level objectives. If the objective is to classify musical instruments by family, the "What Family Does The Instrument Belong To"

SAMPLE VISUALS

The Textures
of Music
HOW MANY
MELODIES?

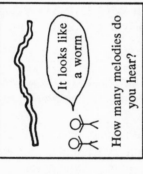

A pack of
worms

How many melodies do
you hear?

Ex. Fugue

It looks like
a worm

How many melodies do
you hear?

Ex. Gregorian chant

Mono = 1
Phonic = Sound
          or
          Voice

Sing by yourself
one melody alone

Ex. Any unaccompanied
songs

Poly = Many
Phonic = Sounds
        or
        Voices

Sing a round
Two songs at once

Ex. Rounds, canons
combinable songs

etc.

Figure 5-4

game can be played by tacking the instrument to the proper section on a chart. Instruments should be identified ultimately by sound. Sight and sound can be combined for presentations and games. If the objective is to classify music by its national origin, a pin (with flag) can be placed in the appropriate country on the map. Flash cards have been used extensively for musical games.

Achieving psychomotor objectives. Motor skills are facilitated by media that can provide models of desired behavior and feedback to the student. For example, students in the instrumental music program must learn to read music and play an instrument. The most obvious and appropriate media for instruction are printed notation and formal or informal instruments. Teachers must further supplement these basic or minimal media with verbal explanations, model demonstrations, outlines, checklists, and/or step-by-step instructions. The tactile, proprioceptive and kinesthetic stimuli are most important. Students must get the physical feel; thus, verbal or written directions are usually inadequate. A demonstration—live, filmed or taped—is effective for guidance and set. The student is guided by the model. He drills or practices what is to be accomplished. Study sheets or rhythms and scales from the music being performed provide the best practice material. It is essential that all etudes, drills and exercises are selected to lead to the attainment of objectives.

The Language-Master audiocard has been used to individualize the learning of rhythmic reading. The system uses a magnetic recording and playback device. A "flash card" contains the written rhythmic pattern to be learned, and a magnetic strip on the lower edge upon which the rhythm has been prerecorded. The student looks at the rhythm and runs the card through the machine to hear it played. Then he records the rhythm and compares it with the prerecorded example.

The video tape recorder can be used to provide the model and feedback to the student for performance analysis. He can view his performance for evaluation and improvement. The tape recorder, electronic tuner and stroboscope can also be used for modeling and feedback. One band director uses an effective strategy to teach students to individually tune their instruments by ear. He uses the

"Lectro-tuner" and "Strobo-tuner" as media. The following steps outline his procedure.

1. Carefully warm up your instrument.
2. Play the tuning note with the tone generator (Lectro-tuner).
3. Listen for beats. The faster the beats, the more out of tune you are.
4. Alternately play the pitch and listen to the tuner. Decide if you are sharp or flat.
5. Adjust tuning slide, barrel or mouthpiece as appropriate for your instrument.
6. Go back to Step Two and continue cycling until all beats are gone.
7. When beats have been eliminated, check tuning visually with the Strobo-tuner.

Achieving affective objectives. Careful choice of media can influence attainment of affective objectives. Films, slides, and recordings chosen for their feelingful impact can shape attitudes, taste and aesthetic perception. The tape recorder and synthesizer provide a means for reaching creative objectives.

Provide Feedback for Modification or Reinforcement

Feedback or formative evaluation should be built into all instruction. Students need feedback for immediate knowledge of results to learn efficiently and effectively. Programed instruction is perhaps the best example, but media can be used extensively to build feedback into all instruction. Several examples will help demonstrate potential uses of media for feedback.

Following the learning module (Figure 5-4), several examples of textures are played for students to classify. The teacher confirms each answer immediately after the students respond by uncovering a prepared transparency to reveal answers one by one.

Self-scoring tests are easy to devise. Fold up the answer sheet and staple it to the question sheets. The test can be taken at any time or place to provide guidance for the student. Directions can be provided on the answer sheet for future learning tasks based upon incorrect answers.

The opaque projector can be used at any school level to project student work in notation, theory or composition. The work can be discussed and evaluated by the class.

The evaluation of skills is best achieved by the video tape recorder. In the conducting class we tape neophyte conductors, then discuss and evaluate the performance privately after class. A rating scale is used to focus upon important behaviors. The audio tape recorder can also be used effectively in concerts or lessons to play back immediately and evaluate the performance for improvement.

The use of media in assessment is discussed further in the next chapter.

Mediated Instruction

The music teacher should strive to effectively utilize the full range of human and nonhuman resources to facilitate learning. Figure 5-5 illustrates the spectrum of possibilities.

At one extreme, mediated instruction provides a viable alternative to traditional instruction. "Mediated instruction" refers to the exclusive use of media in the teaching/learning situation. The medium does the teaching. There is no face-to-face contact with a live teacher. The complete lesson is presented in a mediated form, with all necessary verbal commentary incorporated within it. Educational television, films and programed instruction are good examples. At the other end of the continuum, the teacher does not use any instructional media other than "natural" means of communication. At this point in time, most classroom transactions would seem to be located in between the two extremes. The skilled teacher selects and uses various media as needed to attain the stated objectives. Programed materials, films or television may present part of the lesson in mediated form. The teacher incorporates other media to support his instructional strategies. The trend toward individualized learning seems to indicate an increased use of mediated instruction in the future. Students will learn how to learn by taking

TEACHER/MEDIA CONTINUUM

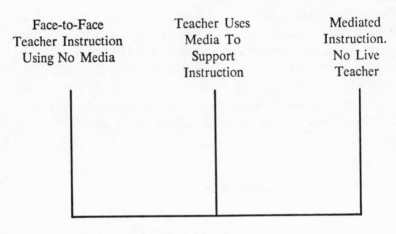

| Face-to-Face Teacher Instruction Using No Media | Teacher Uses Media To Support Instruction | Mediated Instruction. No Live Teacher |

Figure 5-5

a more active role in the selection of learning activities and media to achieve their objectives.

Self-Check Mastery Test

1. What are instructional media? Give examples of various types.
2. What are uses and advantages of the new media in teaching?
3. What are the general criteria for selecting media?
4. What are the levels of media?
5. What are appropriate media for each tactic of the basic teaching strategy?

6

assessing musical
instructional effectiveness

Objectives:

Upon mastering the content of this chapter, the reader should be able to:

1. Describe the function of assessment in the accountability approach.
2. Define and contrast norm-referenced test and criterion-referenced test.
3. Describe the type of information each test yields.
4. Describe how to construct a criterion-referenced test.
5. Write test items for objectives in each of the four major categories.

Assessment is the most essential and conspicuous component of the accountability approach. It is the means of measuring the degree of success of the total instructional operation. Assessment must be built into the system as an integral, continuously functioning part. Perhaps this sounds redundant, but many people seem to regard "testing" and "measurement" as something outside of or in addition to instruction. At worst, testing is an end in itself—the alpha and omega of formal education. Carl Rogers says it quite well:

> Taking examinations and preparing for the next exam is a way of life for students. . . . It has gradually come to be assumed by teachers, students, and parents that report cards and grades *constitute* education. When a faculty member asked a student what he got out of a course, the student's response was what one would expect from this [traditional] system: "I got a B."[1]

Too often the emphasis is upon grades, not learning. However, testing cannot stop with grading.

The primary function of all testing is to provide a basis for decision-making. Assessment answers some very basic instructional questions: Are students achieving the course objectives? To what extent? Are the teaching procedures effective? Is the music program successful? With assessment results teachers can act to improve instruction.

In this chapter norm-referenced tests and criterion-referenced tests are examined to differentiate the nature of information they yield. Guidelines are provided for constructing criterion-referenced tests. Objectives are categorized for assessment. Examples of appropriate test items are included.

Assessment in the Accountability Approach

The accountability approach is primarily concerned with mastery learning. This means that every student should attain the

---

[1] Carl R. Rogers, "The Facilitation of Significant Learning," in *Instruction, Some Contemporary Viewpoints*, Laurence Siegel, ed. (San Francisco: Chandler Publishing Company, 1967), p. 41.

specified musical knowledge, skills and attitudes delineated in the behavioral objectives.

Musical learning has been defined as the acquisition of desired musical behaviors through experience. (See Chapter 2.) Your objectives identify the behaviors that you deem worthy for students to acquire. Assessment determines if the designated behaviors have in fact been acquired. Ascertaining the extent to which each student has achieved objectives provides information to analyze present performance and prescribe the future course for each learner at the end of a unit of instruction. The performance becomes the new entry level for the student. (See Chapter 3.) It supplies the student with the feedback of information necessary for self-evaluation, self-direction, and self-improvement. All are important for learner independence. The student learns how to learn.

Assessment also indicates the degree of instructional effectiveness. From this data decisions can be made about the total functioning of the instructional system and the modifications that are needed in it. Look again at Figure 1-4. Changes and adjustments can be made in objectives, preassessment, procedures, strategies, media and/or evaluation.

In summary, the purpose of assessment is to inform decision-making by providing feedback for modification—improvement of the system and direction for the learner.

Choosing Measurement Instruments

Now you must locate or construct appropriate measurement tools to assess your classes. Two approaches can be taken.

1. Use standardized tests or teacher-made tests with a normal curve distribution ranking of students (norm-referenced measurement).
2. Use tests that provide information about student mastery of specific objectives (criterion-referenced measurement).

The difference between NRM and CRM is a crucial one for accountability. Tests may look similar in construction, format, test items or raw scores. However, the kind of test you should use depends upon the type of information you are seeking. See Figure 6-1

COMPARISON OF TWO TYPES OF MEASUREMENT INSTRUMENTS

	NORM-REFERENCED MEASUREMENT [NRM]	CRITERION-REFERENCED MEASUREMENT [CRM]
Definition (Description) of the test	NRM indicates the relative ranking of an individual with regard to others (norm group) in the subject matter being tested.	CRM indicates the mastery of a specific performance; it provides information about the degree of competence attained by a particular pupil toward achieving specified instructional objectives.
Type of information it yields	NRM discloses how a student compares with others but not the specific things he is able to do.	CRM discloses what each individual can do and the effectiveness of "treatments" (methods of instruction).
What the test does	NRM samples a subject matter area to ascertain knowledge. Objectives are vague.	CRM samples specified performance (behavioral) objectives.
Use of data	NRM can discriminate among pupils to place them in proper grouping, to select the best for special training, to limit enrollment, to give grades, to predict success, to determine long term or overall achievement.	CRM determines degree of competency prior, during and/or after instruction; measures mastery learning; assesses short term learning modules and units.

Figure 6-1

	NRM	CRM
Status of pupil	NRM indicates relative status.	CRM indicates absolute status, according to the criterion (standard).
How reported	NRM is reported in stanine scores, percentile scores or grade equivalents.	CRM is reported as pass-fail (achieved mastery or didn't) percent of correct answers (p-scores), or ratio (90-90).
Types of test items (item analysis)	NRM retains those items that discriminate best among pupils of high and low ability.	CRM retains items that accurately reflect the performance objective that they assess.
Variability	NRM must have a spread of scores to discriminate among pupils. A normal curve is expected.	In CRM, spread is irrelevant. Hope that all students achieve high scores at the end of the instructional sequence.
Reliability	NRM should be consistent for individuals. Test-retest, split half or equivalent forms are used.	CRM should be consistent also, but usual reliability methods are difficult to apply. Anticipate much difference between pre- and posttest scores in a positive direction.
Validity	In NRM, determined by statistical validity (correlation with outside criteria) or content validity.	In CRM, *must* have content validity.
Objectivity	NRM should yield uniform scores regardless who grades the test.	CRM should yield uniform scores regardless who grades the test.

Figure 6-1 (cont.)

for a "quick" comparison. The following discussion is more detailed.

Norm-Referenced Tests

The norm-referenced test provides a sample of subject matter attainment by ranking students in the order of most proficient to least proficient. It assigns a student to a percentile rank, stanine score, or grade level that indicates his relative standing in a specified population (norm-group). Thus it is possible to compare one individual with another individual or one group with another group in terms of relative status. Since scores are of a comparative nature, however, you cannot tell from this data exactly what a student knows or what he can do. Because of this limitation standardized tests are often inappropriate to assess a specific course.

A teacher's course objectives and their possible incompatibility with item analysis techniques create further problems. To "standardize" a test it must be administered to groups of specified backgrounds and experience to establish norms. Questions are selected in the tryouts for their appropriate difficulty and discriminating power. Test items are eliminated if they are answered by too many or too few students. As a result many questions relevant to course objectives may be eliminated through item-selection techniques because they do not discriminate well between high-ability and low-ability pupils.

Using standardized tests for accountability can be statistically inappropriate. The average is established by the median score of the norm group, the fiftieth percentile. It means that one-half of the students upon whom the test was standardized scored above and one-half scored below. Teachers are often held accountable for at least the "average" score for all their pupils. Yet, by definition, this is a statistical impossibility.

Even teacher-made tests that make use of normal distribution or ranking procedures may not be appropriate for assessing achievement. For example, an average score is, by definition, acceptable since it defines a "standard." It describes the actual performance of the group. Accountability in this sense is easy. Flanagan explains it this way:

> . . . "standard" implies something set up as a desirable model or minimum goal, whereas "norm" carries the connotation of describing things as they actually are. It seems unwise to encourage a usage which tends without criticism and automatically to establish the present average performance of individuals on a test (the "norm") as the acceptable score (the "standard") for the test.[2]

In a similar way the normal distribution creates problems for the slower learners. The approach guarantees that some will fail, even if their scores, though the lowest in class, may be adequate for a particular task. It promotes cheating, unhealthy competition, frustration and discipline problems.

Before examining an alternative procedure, consider positive uses for norm-referenced tests. The information they provide is valuable for certain purposes: 1) To select the best available talent when there are few openings in an organization. The director of an advanced performing group may wish to limit enrollment and audition students to determine the most proficient. 2) To compare individuals on a trait or skill. Sectional tryouts in performing groups are held to rank students from best to worst and assign them to appropriate chairs. 3) To predict success. Aptitude tests are often used to choose students for beginning instrumental instruction, especially if the class has too many applicants. (The validity of this testing is often suspect.) On the other hand, aptitude tests may be given to the total student body to determine the best prospects for musical training. 4) To assign grades at the end of a term. A normal curve distribution is used to insure the full range of marks.

Since norm-referenced testing is not suitable for accountability assessment, it will not be pursued further.

Criterion-Referenced Tests

The purpose of criterion-referenced testing in the accountability model is to measure the attainment of specific instructional objec-

---

[2] John C. Flanagan "Units, Scores, and Norms" in *Educational Measurement,* B. F. Lindquist, ed. (Washington, D.C.: American Council on Education, 1951), p. 700.

tives. Criterion-referenced testing ascertains an individual's standing not in relation to others but in regard to predetermined performance standards—the mastery of specified instructional objectives. The test items correspond directly to the objectives. There is at least one test item for every objective.

Since the criterion-referenced test clearly states what a pupil is able to do in behavioral terms, it provides the only acceptable means of assessing instruction. It is the principal measurement tool of accountability. A good instructional strategy, then, is to construct the criterion-referenced test at the time you develop the desired course objectives, and actively *teach toward it*!

Teach for the Test?

Mention was made earlier that teachers have reasons to be upset when a standardized test is used indiscriminately as a measure of accountability. The test may not reflect the objectives that the teacher is committed to facilitating. Yet his students, hence his teaching, will be evaluated with this instrument. The pragmatic thing to do in this case is to teach for the test. Two problems arise: one concerns ethics; the other objectives.

1. We have long heard that it is unethical to teach for a test. It is cheating—similar to a student stealing an examination. Note, however, that a "test" in this case is a small sample of knowledge, and teaching for the specific items would not result in complete or comprehensive learning of the subject by the student.
2. When you teach for a test, the test dictates your objectives. You are stuck with the questions that the test asks. These test items must be converted into your instructional objectives.

The reaction to both of these situations is usually one of rebellion and rejection of achievement testing. Yet rejection is no answer. It results in situations we have all experienced, especially at the university level. The teachers "teach;" that is, lecture. At the end of the grading period they give a test so that students can get their grades. The test, however, does not really correspond to what has been taught. How could fifty true-false items or some obscure essay questions be what the instructors taught? Even they deny it. Students are bewildered, and the teachers do not know what students have really gained from the lectures and discussions. Whatever they taught evidently cannot be tested. They refuse to be accountable.

The accountability approach provides an alternative solution. Don't reject achievement tests or rework standardized tests into objectives. Instead, carefully write behavioral objectives and construct criterion-referenced tests to measure their achievement. Then teach for the test. If the test really is a statement of your objectives, do not be ashamed of doing this. If most students get all the questions correct—rejoice!! This is what you are striving for. It shows that you are a good teacher.

Restate Objectives as Test Questions?

By and large students study for tests, especially if grades are given. From the student's point of view, the tests that an instructor gives indicate the real objectives of a course. Even if a statement of course objectives is provided, students attempt to "psych out" the teacher to determine his test forms, questions, idiosyncrasies, and generally to find out "what does he want" to get a high grade.

To capitalize in a positive way upon this potent motivating force, many successful teachers provide students with sample questions, rating scales and even complete tests. The following listening test, used in college music appreciation courses, was distributed to students at the first class meeting as a statement of course objectives. (Enroute behaviors were subtested and some cognitive content was included to evaluate important concepts and information.)

Example 1

Music 111   FINAL EXAMINATION

Listen to the recorded excerpts and identify the musical elements of tonality, meter, texture and tone color for each. Also classify each example by historical style period. Format of answer:

Tonality: tonal, atonal
Rhythm: metrical, nonmetrical
Texture: monophonic, homophonic, polyphonic
Timbre: name of musical group (orchestra, band, chorus, string quartet, woodwind quintet) or solo instrument
Historical Style Period: Renaissance, Baroque, Classical, Romantic, Contemporary

The adjudicators form is another good example of a test that can be provided for students as a statement of objectives and that you can teach toward in your performing groups. The items for rating are included, but students must accomplish them within the context of each composition they perform. Put a large copy of the adjudication items on the front wall of the rehearsal room so that it faces the students. Working for this "test" should result in better performance.

Writing Test Items

The criterion-referenced test consists of the specific tasks or test items that you will accept as evidence that objectives have been attained. These test items should be constructed at the same time that behavioral objectives are written.

As a test constructor, try to visualize exactly what a student should be doing when he is successfully achieving the objective. As much as possible, the test item or task should engage the student in the *same* performance that the instructional objective requires. Testing need not be limited to paper-and-pencil activities. Playing, singing, notating, and demonstrating can all be formal test behaviors. Testing can also be informal. You can informally talk to students and ask questions, or observe their present performance level.

The approach at this point should be wide open and creative. Try to figure out the best way even if it requires novel approaches. Reserve judgment. That wild idea may turn out to be the springboard to the best way to test. For example, one junior high band director I know used cassette tape recorders to assess achievement of prescribed material. Students went singly during the full rehearsal to tape in an adjacent practice room. He evaluated the tapes during his free period.

NAEP (National Assessment of Educational Progress) has developed criterion-referenced measures which they call exercises. An "exercise" is a task which is written to measure an objective. This term is used instead of test item since their approach to assessment is often open ended, using interviews, performances and other tasks. Some NAEP exercises can be given in group situations; others must be administered individually.[3]

As stated earlier in the chapter, objectives and measurement criteria have assessment value only if developed and used together. The IOX Music Objectives provide good illustrations of this concept.[4] The collection includes: (1) the objective, (2) a measurement item, and (3) a means for judging the adequacy of student responses.

Example 2

IOX Objective 58

OBJECTIVE:	Given an aural presentation of vocal or instrumental compositions in simple song form, the [grade 4-6 general music] student will identify correctly its form.
SAMPLE ITEM:	Listen to the composition, "The Wild Horseman." Identify the form of the composition through rhythmic movement.
ANSWER:	1. Form is ABA
	2. Exact repetition of movement used for the two parts of A
	3. Contrast in movement for part B

Constructing the Criterion-Referenced Test

Since the traditional rules of test construction are difficult to apply to criterion-referenced testing, some guidelines are presented to

---

[3] See Carmen J. Finley and Frances S. Berdie, *The National Assessment Approach To Exercise Development* (Ann Arbor, Michigan: NAEP, 1970).

[4] *Instructional Objectives Exchange*, Music K-6 (Los Angeles: Center For The Study Of Evaluation, UCLA, 1969).

help get you started. The discussion relies heavily upon the NAEP approach.

Content Validity

Validity in the traditional sense means that a test actually measures what it purports to measure. The criterion-referenced test must be subjected to a judgment of content validity. Does it really test the objective or does it test something else? The approach is rather obvious and requires common sense. The test question must relate specifically to the objective to be a valid item. According to NAEP,

> An exercise has content validity if it is a direct measure of some important bit of knowledge, skill or attitude that reflects one or more objectives of a subject area. An exercise must be meaningful, make sense and be directly related to the objective. It must not be trivial, inconsequential or peripheral to the objective. In practice, then, an exercise has content validity if it makes sense to an informed reader who sees it together with the objective and says, "Yes, this [is] a good measure of the knowledge or skill called for by this objective."[5]

Clarity

The student must be able to understand the question. Often it is advisable to read the directions and questions for the student. Otherwise the question must be written clearly and on the vocabulary level of the student. Test items should further be written in concise, simple and direct language. Clarity can best be determined by trying out the test and making an item analysis before using it extensively. (Remember that if an item does not "discriminate," it need not be dropped as long as it reflects an important attribute of the objective.)

---

[5] Finley and Berdie, *The National Assessment Approach To Exercise Development*, p. 15.

Form

The objectives may suggest the best form for structuring a question. Mention was made earlier of creative and novel approaches. For example, one music teacher suggested using MMO (Music Minus One) recordings for better evaluating individual music-reading ability. *The Evaluation of Music Teaching and Learning* by Richard Colwell contains a wealth of suggestions.[6]

Survey the best ways to ask the questions and structure the test tasks. The following list illustrates some possible test forms.

1. Information examinations
    a. true-false
    b. multiple choice
    c. matching
    d. completion
    e. short answer
    d. essay
2. Listening tests
3. Student reports
    a. book reports
    b. musical analyses
    c. project report
    d. research paper
    e. term paper
4. Interview
    a. oral examination
    b. conference
5. Performance measures
    a. rating scales
    b. check lists
    c. adjudicators form
    d. videotape scales
    e. tryout
    f. applied examinations (juries)
6. Activity inventories (what do you do, collect, etc.?)

---

[6] (Englewood Cliffs, N.J.: Prentice-Hall, Inc., 1970).

    a.   books
    b.   records
    c.   practice routine
    d.   listening habits
    e.   music file

7. Anecdotal records
8. Student logs
9. Direct observation (informal)
10. Self-evaluation
11. Attitude scale or opinionnaire

Time Allotment

The length of time needed for administering a test can be a major constraint in test construction because music periods and rehearsals are usually limited. For example, a one-hundred-piece band is a difficult situation in which to evaluate individual sight-reading ability. Listening to each student would require at least six class periods. Innovations are needed to assess many important objectives. Various out-of-class tests can be used to supplement those given during class hours. The tape recorder can help.

Criterion Level and Grading

You must determine how tasks should be graded and recorded. Again, the approach is different from norm-referenced testing, both for individuals and for groups.

For an individual student, the common practice is to decide upon a minimum acceptable score. This is often an arbitrary procedure on the part of the instructor. Experience can be a guide. As a rule of thumb, 85 or 90 percent is accepted as the criterion score. Since "mastery learning" demands individual achievement, every student should be expected to attain this level or be recycled through the instructional system. Research studies have shown that *time* is the critical variable—given enough time, all students can master the objectives. I have used this recycling approach with programed study materials in musical form. The students who did not achieve the 90 percent on the posttest restudied the material and "corrected" their own test until they built up the necessary percentage points.

Check lists and rating scales are appropriate measurement tools for assessing skills. When you are primarily interested in determining if the desired behavior has *in fact* been exhibited, you can check items off as they are mastered—pass or no-pass. (See Example 3.)

Example 3

Conducting I, Assessment   Date of
                                                           Attainment

11. Demonstrate the *fermata* on all beats
    and divisions of beats required by the
    musical example and/or required by
    the instructor:
    a. with complete release and sub-
       sequent preparatory beat   _____
    b. with the release gesture used as
       a preparatory beat   _____
    c. without release but with a pre-
       paratory gesture for resumption   _____

Example 3 represents three items from a twenty-five item check list of basic conducting skills. The accumulation of items on the complete assessment instrument results in a multibehavior criterion test for the course. Since each task is graded on a pass or no-pass basis, the criterion level for the complete test can be set wherever it seems appropriate: at 85, 90 or 100 percent. I think all of the tasks are essential for the conductor, so I withhold a student's grade until he achieves all of them.

Perhaps you desire more discrimination than a pass-fail check list affords. For example, you may want to assign students to different groups according to skill level at the end of the present instructional sequence. Use a rating scale to determine how well each student performs on a single objective. As in cognitive objectives, most skill objectives can have a range of acceptable performance. You can use a five-point scale to indicate how well a student sings or plays a particular passage relative to stated objectives. Applied to Example 3, the rating scale defines levels of ability to conduct a *fermata* by grade (A, B, C, D, E) or by numerical value (1, 2, 3, 4, 5). A definition or model description of each level should be supplied so that raters can agree. The criterion level is then set for the attainment of each objective. For example, a "2" rating on a five-point scale is acceptable.

Traditional descriptive statistics can be used for reporting group test scores. However, "means" and "standard deviations" are most appropriate for norm-referenced measurement. The simplest and most meaningful way of reporting group scores is to indicate the percentage of students who correctly answered the item. This is called a p-value or p-score by NAEP. It conversely reveals the percentage of students who have not reached criterion level. Finally, a proportion can be used as an index of pupil attainment. The 90-90 criterion is often used for programed instructional material. It means that at least 90 percent of the students obtained at least a 90 percent score.

In the accountability approach, there can be no normal distribution of grades as in norm-referenced measurement. A successful course will result in a skewed curve and almost all "A" grades. If all students attain the objectives how can it be any other way?

The Test Plan

A test plan should be followed to insure that all important variables have been considered. Such a plan can include: what to test, when to test, what type of questions, what format, what length of test, and other practical considerations. Several points need special emphasis.

1. List objectives to be sure each is represented in the test.
   a. This eliminates the possibility of testing only the lowest levels of learning. Evaluate test items and objectives against criteria as the Bloom Taxonomy.[7]

---

[7] Benjamin S. Bloom, et al., *Taxonomy of Educational Objectives: The Classification of Educational Goals. Handbook I: Cognitive Domain* (New York: David McKay Co., Inc., 1956).

2. Weight objectives in relative importance.
   a. Tests that include more than one objective are multibehavioral.
   b. Emphasize important objectives by developing and using more items for them.
3. Check the time needed for answering each item, to assure feasibility.

Classifying and Measuring Musical Objectives

Objectives can be classified in many ways. Bloom and others have utilized taxonomies.[8] Concepts have served as a basis for several sets of musical objectives; e.g., the California State Music Objectives. Musical activities provide a third framework around which musical objectives can be structured. Regardless of initial approach, most musical objectives can be classified in one of four basic categories for measurement: 1) knowledge, 2) aural perception, 3) motor performance, and 4) affective response. Each area suggests appropriate modes of evaluation.

Assessing Knowledge Objectives

Knowledge and associated cognitive operations encompass the objectives that relate to the recognition or recall and classification of musical symbols (notation), musical vocabulary, and information about musical elements, forms, historical styles, composers, compositions, musical functions, etc.

Knowledge, especially "memory," is easily tested in a group situation. Assessing knowledge requires verbal or symbolic responses. Any pencil-and-paper, objective test format is applicable. Multiple-choice format is especially appropriate because of objectivity and convenience of grading.

---

[8] Bloom, *op. cit.*, David R. Krathwohl, et al., *Taxonomy of Educational Objectives: The Classification of Educational Goals Handbook II: Affective Domain* (New York: David McKay Co., Inc., 1956, and Elizabeth Jane Simpson, *The Classification of Educational Objectives, Psychomotor Domain* (Urbana: University of Illinois, 1966).

Since it is easy to test for information, assessment of knowledge objectives tends to be overdone. The lowest level and least important musical objectives fall in this category.

Example 4

OBJECTIVE: Given musical notation at his level of instruction, the [grade 3-4] student will identify the letter names of the notes on the treble staff at least 90% accuracy.

SAMPLE ITEM: On the line below each pitch that is written on your answer sheet, write the letter name of each pitch.

Example 5

OBJECTIVE: Given a list of prominent composers, the student will identify the major historical style period in which each composed with 90% accuracy.

SAMPLE ITEM: On the line preceding the name of each composer, write the historical style period in which he composed.

_____	Mozart	_____	Haydn
_____	Brahms	_____	Schoenberg
_____	Wagner	_____	Handel
_____	Stravinsky	_____	Berlioz
_____	Bach	_____	Copland

Example 6

OBJECTIVE: Given the notation to a sequence of notes, at his level of instruction, the student will describe the sequence in terms

TEST ITEM:
of its movement up, down, or remaining the same.

There are six short musical motives on your answer sheet. On the line below each example write DOWN— if the melody moves down, UP—if the melody moves upward, or write SAME—if the pitches of the melody remain the same.

Example 7

OBJECTIVE:
Given the period names, the senior high school instrumental music student will place the five major historical periods of music in chronological order.

SAMPLE ITEM:
The five major periods of music chronologically 1450 to the present time are:

a. Classical, Baroque, Renaissance, Romantic, Contemporary

b. Renaissance, Classical, Baroque, Romantic, Contemporary

c. Renaissance, Baroque, Classical, Romantic, Contemporary

d. Renaissance, Baroque, Romantic, Classical, Contemporary

e. Renaissance, Romantic, Baroque, Classical, Contemporary

Assessing Aural Perception Objectives

Perceptual awareness requires the application of knowledge and the classification of musical stimuli. It couples musical perception with cognitive operations to classify musical elements, forms, historical styles, composers, compositions, musical functions, etc. Such objectives can include the recognition of musical instruments, the direction of melodic movement, and errors of intonation, balance, rhythm and notation. Attainment of perceptual objectives is important for both general students and music students.

Fortunately, it is easy to generate test items for these objectives and therefore easy to assess their mastery. Music listening tests in general music, music appreciation and music literature classes are good examples. Audio stimuli are needed to accompany the pencil-and-paper format.

Example 8

OBJECTIVE: Upon hearing examples of recorded music in which a different solo instrument is predominant, the learner will identify the solo instrument by sound with at least 70% accuracy.

SAMPLE ITEM: Write the name of the solo instrument that you hear, for each example, on your answer sheet.

1._____   4._____

2._____   5._____

3._____   6._____

Example 9

OBJECTIVE: Upon hearing musical examples, at his level of instruction, the learner will identify each as (1) monody, (2) polyphony, (3) block harmony, or (4) accompanied melody, with at least 75% accuracy.

SAMPLE ITEM: Write the appropriate number on your answer sheet for each example you hear.

(1)   Monody—only one melodic line

(2)   Polyphony—more than one melodic line

(3)   Block Harmony—all voices moving at the same time.

(4)   Accompanied Melody—one melodic

line with a harmonic accompaniment.

1.＿＿＿ 4.＿＿＿ 7.＿＿＿
2.＿＿＿ 5.＿＿＿ 8.＿＿＿
3.＿＿＿ 6.＿＿＿ 9.＿＿＿

Example 10

OBJECTIVE: Upon hearing musical examples, characteristic of a certain style period, the student will name the specific period with at least 70% accuracy.

SAMPLE ITEM: After hearing each musical excerpt, place the letter which best describes the music in the space on your answer sheet.

A. Renaissance D. Romantic
B. Baroque E. Impressionist
C. Classical F. Contemporary

1.＿＿＿ 4.＿＿＿ 7.＿＿＿
2.＿＿＿ 5.＿＿＿ 8.＿＿＿
3.＿＿＿ 6.＿＿＿

Example 11

OBJECTIVE: Given recorded examples of triads played by orchestral instruments, the high school instrumental music student will identify intonation descrepancies in each chord.

SAMPLE ITEM: In the three-note chord you just heard the
a. bottom note was flat
b. middle note was sharp
c. middle note was flat
d. upper note was sharp
e. triad was in tune

Example 12

OBJECTIVE: Given recorded examples of triads played by orchestral instruments, the high school instrumental student will identify balance problems in each chord.

SAMPLE ITEM: In the three-note chord you have just heard the
- a. bottom note was too loud
- b. bottom note was too soft
- c. middle note was too loud
- d. upper note was too soft
- e. triad was balanced.

Assessing Motor Skill Objectives

Motor performance requires the application of knowledge through physical response. It includes the skills of singing, playing instruments and music reading. This category of objectives requires assessment through individual testing. You can utilize informal observation, or formal observation with rating scales, check lists or score cards. Audio and video tape recordings have been successfully used for skill assessment in instrumental performance, conducting, and dramatic productions. More innovative approaches are needed to facilitate individual evaluation of large numbers of students.

Example 13

OBJECTIVE: Upon hearing simple rhythm patterns, the student will imitate them by clapping or playing a rhythm instrument with at least 90% accuracy.

SAMPLE ITEM: Imitate the rhythm that the teacher claps. Teacher claps:

Student echoes pattern.

Example 14

OBJECTIVE: Given measures of rhythmic notation, at his level of instruction, the student will

perform the rhythmic pattern by clapping, chanting, or playing an instrument with at least 90% accuracy.

SAMPLE ITEM: Clap the following rhythm patterns in the tempo established by the teacher.

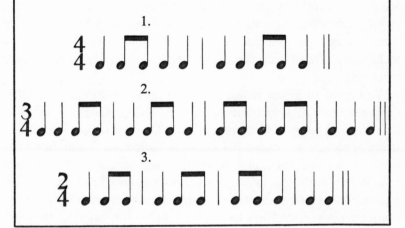

Example 15

OBJECTIVE: 6. Starting on any prescribed yard line of a football field, the bandsman will demonstrate his ability to march fifty yards using eight steps to every five yards without error while playing movement music a M.M. 130 (by the third week of rehearsal).

TEST ITEM: Start on the_____ yard line and play_____ music while marching 8 to 5 for fifty yards. Attention! Forward march!

CRITERION: Observe each bandsman perform individually; or observe squads perform and check each individual; or observe a company front of all or part of the marching band and check who does not meet the criterion.

Assessing Affective Objectives

Affective learnings are the most important outcomes of the music program and the most difficult to assess. The affective domain includes musical creativity, discrimination, preferences, attitudes, and aesthetic sensitivity. Evaluating affective objectives remains a largely subjective operation, but guidelines can be provided. Innovation is again needed to develop nonreactive, observational techniques. Otherwise we must settle for easily faked verbal responses.

You can best assess attitudes toward music classes and the music program through systematic surveys involving students, classroom teachers and parents. Construct observation and survey instruments using approach-avoidance behaviors as indicators. Set up items that can be answered yes/no or rated on an intensity scale. Supplement this with a daily log in which you record anecdotal observations and comments. One affective outcome for which most music teachers strive is for students to enjoy (like, prize, love) their music classes. The following outline can be used as a basis for an attitude survey that provides feedback from students, teachers and parents.

Feedback from students. You can observe students informally or use a check list to determine their attitude. Obviously, all of the items will not apply to all of the students. However, a composite of items will indicate the direction of student feelings. Find out if students:

1. Elect music classes and musical activities when they have other alternatives
2. Regularly attend all classes, performances and extra rehearsals
3. Participate in extra musical activities as ensembles, solos, festivals, honors groups, all-city, etc.
4. Initiate musical activities
5. Do extra class work voluntarily
6. Arrange schedule to accommodate musical activities
7. Seek help in musical endeavors
8. Voluntarily attend concerts and other musical programs
9. Help or work in the music room
10. Hang around the music room

Feedback from classroom teachers. Teachers often volunteer positive and negative information about music. Give them some items like the following to help systematically survey attitudes. Do students:

1. Want to go to music class?
2. Eagerly anticipate music class?
3. Talk enthusiastically about music class?
4. Inform the teacher about activities in music?
5. Want to continue musical activities in the classroom?
6. Want to perform for the class?
7. Talk their friends into joining musical activities?

Feedback from parents. Parents usually report extreme reactions to some phase of the music program, as high praise or adamant disagreement. A survey will bring in more objective data to use for evaluation. Ask parents if students:

1. Talk enthusiastically about school music
2. Talk about musical programs, concerts, activities
3. Sing songs learned in school
4. Practice instruments voluntarily
5. Take private music lessons
6. Participate in out-of-school music: church, dance bands, recreational, civic
7. Voluntarily attend concerts and other musical programs
8. Listen to recordings (What kinds?)
9. Read books about music and musicians
10. Talk about music as a vocation

Assessing creativity, musical preference and aesthetic sensitivity is more difficult but not impossible. Creativity, for example, can be fostered and evaluated using such guidelines as developed by the Manhattanville Music Curriculum Project.[9] Example 16 sets up formal specifications to assist evaluation of creative projects used to develop musical competencies of general elementary teachers. The other examples assess preference and aesthetic outcomes.

---

[9] Ronald B. Thomas, *Synthesis, A Structure For Music Education* (Elnora, N.Y.: Media, Inc. 1970).

Example 16

Project #2 (Basic Task)
Compose a melody, notate it, and perform it on the piano.
Specifications:
1. Use various notes in the treble clef in any combination that is pleasing and satisfying to you.
2. Use at least a total of twenty-four notes.
3. Notate on manuscript paper in the treble clef.
4. Notate pitches only (you do not have to indicate note values in this project, unless you wish to do so).
5. Begin and end on the same note.
6. Try not to repeat consecutive notes too often.
7. Perform accurately on the piano.

Example 17

(Inferring Personal Preference, IOX—#56)

OBJECTIVE: Given listening selections in which there are contrasting sections, the student will indicate his feeling preferences by responding to written statements about the various sections of the music.

SAMPLE ITEM: Instructions to teacher: Play the piece of music "The Red Pony" for the students. After the performance have the student check the statements which most clearly describe his feelings and reactions to the music.
1. I like the second part of the music—
   ( ) better than the first part
   ( ) not as well as the first part
2. I like both parts—
   ( ) not at all
   ( ) the same
   ( ) very much

CRITERIA: The student will indicate his own musical preferences.

Example 18

(Inferring Aesthetic Response)

OBJECTIVE: The student perceives the expressive line of music's undulation through patterns of intensity to release.

TEST ITEM: In the example you just heard, the musical intensity

        a. increased to climax, then decreased to cadence.

        b. increased and decreased several times with little climax.

        c. increased gradually and ended at the climax point.

Self-Check Mastery Test

1. What is the function of assessment in the accountability approach?
2. What is a norm-referenced test?
3. What is a criterion-referenced test?
4. What is the difference between the two types of tests? What kind of information or data does each test yield?
5. How do you construct a criterion-referenced test?
6. Write test items for the following objectives and/or objectives that you use in your classes.
    a. Given a notated rhythm pattern, the student will perform the pattern, accenting the first beat of each measure.
    b. Upon hearing a series of musical phrases, e.g., several songs, the student will indicate the cadence points (points of relative repose).
    c. Given pictures of standard orchestral instruments, the student will name them by sight with 90 percent accuracy.
    d. Given aural examples of concert music that the class has studied, the student will indicate his preferences.

Guidelines and sample test items for Question 6.

Objective "a" Guidelines: The category is motor skill. You must provide a suitable rhythm pattern for the student's reading level. Student must clap (play on a drum, etc.) the rhythm for you, or tape record his rendition for you to check later.

Sample Item: Clap the following pattern accenting the first count of each measure:

Objective "b" Guidelines: The category is aural perception. You must provide musical examples (recorded, played on an instrument, or sung) that have strong cadence points.

Sample Item: Listen to the song(s). Raise your hand each time the music reaches a cadence (stopping point).

Objective "c" Guidelines: The category is knowledge. You must provide appropriate pictures of orchestral instruments for the instructional level of the student.

Sample Item: Write the names of the instruments pictured below, in the appropriate space on the answer sheet.

Objective "d" Guidelines: The category is affective. You should not directly ask students for preferences in this type of situation. Rather, you should infer them from candid remarks, physical response, facial expression, movement and gesture. Use a check list or log of individual student responses, or tape record the session without the students' prior knowledge for later analysis.

7

putting the system into

operation in music classes

Objectives

Upon mastering the content of this chapter, the reader should be able to:

1. Outline the four phases and the eight steps of the systems approach to instructional development.
2. Apply the systems approach to music teaching.
3. Write a performance contract.
4. Describe ways to manage systematic teaching.

The preceding chapters have presented the component parts of the accountability model independently for close scrutiny. However, as stated in Chapter 1, the complete system is a synthesis of the elements and gains its strength from the synthesis. Thus the unassembled components can never result in accountability. In this chapter we reassemble the component parts and develop a procedure for putting the system into operation. Performance contracting is investigated as a tactic for instituting accountability. Finally, some suggestions are made for managing systematic instruction (keeping student records and reporting pupil progress).

Systems Approach for Accountable Programs

The systems approach to instructional development is presented here as a summary and application of the preceding chapters. It is, further, a problem-solving technique that can be applied to any effective program of curriculum development. The step-by-step procedure should help you put the accountability system to work in your music teaching. The flow chart (Figure 7-1) provides a model of this process. Stated as simply as possible, you develop behavioral objectives, assessment items, an entry test, procedures and media; you try out the procedures and media selected to achieve the objectives; you systematically assess the effectiveness of instruction by pretesting and posttesting; and you modify the system on the basis of assessment results. There is a design phase, an implementation phase, an assessment phase and a recycling phase.

Figure 7-2 is a worksheet that can be used in the design phase to help focus attention on the important considerations. Every objective and subobjective should be carried through the systems approach. While the worksheet may look like a good old-fashioned lesson plan at first glance, its strength comes from the greater precision of formulation and systematic modification through feedback.

The complete process of the accountability model is first outlined below, then described as a series of steps you can follow.

Design Phase: Specify objectives that identify learner performance.
Develop a criterion test and an entry test.
Select or develop procedures and media to achieve objectives.

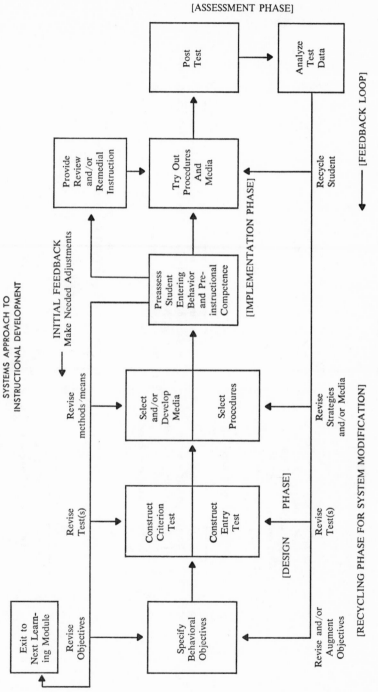

SYSTEMS APPROACH TO
INSTRUCTIONAL DEVELOPMENT

Figure 7-1

WORKSHEET FOR SYSTEMS PLANNING

Course Objective ("Terminal" performance) or

Sub-Objective (Performance that leads to course objective)

Assessment (Criterion-referenced exit tests—pre and post)

What are the specific "test-item" performances you will accept as indicators of student achievement (and of instructional effectiveness)?

Entry Test (Entering behavior)

What are the competencies and/or content prerequisite to obtaining the objective stated above?

What review is needed?

Learning Experience (Learning tasks, instructional strategies, procedures, methods)

	What will the student do?		What will the teacher do?		Methods
	Activities (Learning Tasks)		*Instructional Strategies*		
1.	Interaction with media	1.	Present and clarify objectives	1.	Lecture
2.	Interaction with teacher	2.	Secure and maintain commitment to objectives	2.	Demonstration
3.	Interaction wih other pupils			3.	Discussion
4.	Practice	3.	Review needed prerequisite learning	4.	Discovery
5.	Self-evaluation (feedback)			5.	Problem solving
		4.	Provide situations and activities that lead to objectives (practice)	6.	Question & Inquiry
		5.	Provide for individualized learning	7.	Gaming
		6.	Provide feedback		

Instructional Media

What books, music, materials, musical equipment and/or A-V hardware are needed for student interaction?

Figure 7-2

Implementation Phase: Preassess preinstructional knowledge
of objectives and student entering behavior.
Try out procedures and instructional media.
Assessment Phase: Posttest to measure results of instruction.
Analyze and interpret test data.
Recycling Phase: Modify the system on the basis of the data
analysis.

Step One—Specify Behavioral Objectives

The delineation of objectives is a difficult process. You must consider student characteristics, needs, interests and level; the demands
of society, cultural considerations, philosophical issues and the
higher-level goals of education; and the subject-matter discipline
of music. From general goal statements, learning objectives are
written in precise, operational form in terms of student behavior for
instruction and assessment. The five-point format includes: 1) characteristic student (target population), 2) action verb (observable
behavior), 3) subject-matter content of music, 4) conditions, and
5) performance standards. Target population refers to the grade
level, class, or student group to which the objective is addressed. The
terminal objective must tell explicitly what the student will be able
to do at the end of instruction that he couldn't do before. This includes the response object—the musical, subject-matter with which
he is involved, such as melody, rhythm, notation or historical style.
It should include the conditions under which the student is to perform. It should also indicate how well the student is expected to
perform. Subobjectives are often required in order for the learner
to achieve the terminal objective. Each must be considered in the
systematic sequence. (See Chapter 2.)

Mention has been made of the systems approach as a problem-
solving process. A clear and precise statement of objectives is a
simple way to define the curricular problem. The objective
describes what needs to be done. Test your objectives to determine
if they do in fact define a problem, or if they simply indicate a
method. It has been suggested that the best way to arrive at the
basic and real objective is to keep asking the question, "Why?"
Often we discover that we do things simply because they have al-

ways been done, but we have lost sight of their original purpose. For example, an objective can be written for a student to play a major scale. Why? To help him get the feel of tonality so that he can play music in that key. The objective can now be written: The student will demonstrate his understanding for key by playing scales and etudes in that key. Why? The real "end" is to be able to perform *music* in that key.

Sometimes methodology is important in learning. In this event process objectives are stated to emphasize the way things are to be done. Problem solving and discovery methods are examples of process objectives. Other objectives emphasize a product or behavioral outcome.

Step Two—Develop the Criterion Test and the Entry Test

The criterion test should be constructed at the same time that objectives are written. It consists of the specific test items that you will accept as evidence that this learning has occurred. Items or exercises are derived directly from the stated objectives. Although behavioral objectives do not always provide a test question, they do imply test items which are appropriate to sample student achievement.

The primary function of the criterion-referenced test is that of a posttest, or end-of-unit measure. The same test or an alternative form is also used as a pretest to determine which objectives the student can already achieve prior to instruction. Decide on the minimum score acceptable for mastery. 85 percent has been a rule-of-thumb score for paper-and-pencil tests. In many cases it will be a simple "pass" or "no-pass" indication. That is, the student demonstrates the behavior or he doesn't. The criterion is part of a well-written objective.

The entry test, on the other hand, measures the prerequisite capabilities necessary to achieve objectives. Often entering behavior is assumed or equated with student group characteristics such as grade level or chronological age. The instructional system will fail at this point if pupils lack background proficiency. Therefore, you must construct a test to determine if the student is ready to undertake the proposed learning task. When formal testing is inappropriate, you can informally observe student performance, ask questions or discuss the new unit of study to ascertain entry level. The "tryout" is a good example of an entry test long used in music teaching. (See Chapter 3.)

Step Three—Select or Develop Procedures and Media

Your objectives communicate what each student is expected to be able to do at the end of instruction. Now you must choose appropriate activities, materials and media to achieve them. In what tasks should students be engaged? With what media should they interact to provide or support learning experiences? A well-written objective should suggest many alternative learning tasks and instructional media from which final selections can be made in the problem-solving process. Cost effectiveness, efficiency, resource constraints and availability are several important criteria to be applied after alternatives have been generated.

Planning must also include the optimal grouping of students. Do strategies call for individual, small-group, or large-group instruction? Scheduling of needed time in appropriate time blocks is another related consideration. (See Chapters 4 and 5.)

Step Four—Preassess Student Competencies

Give the criterion-referenced pretest and the entry test. Instruct students to scan the tests before attempting them, and then to answer only what they feel they can. Explain the diagnostic function of this assessment. *It will not affect grades.* Assign students to appropriate learning tasks on the basis of the test results. Preassessment should indicate if students already have mastered some of the objectives or if they lack prerequisite competencies. In the former situation, they should be moved ahead to appropriate advanced tasks; in the latter situation, review or remedial instruction is necessary before they can undertake the proposed tasks. It is possible that this initial feedback will require a complete revision of objectives, tests, methods and/or media. (See the first feedback loop in Figure 7-1.)

Step Five—Try Procedures and Media

If preassessment has confirmed the anticipated entry level, you are ready to try out the teaching strategies and instructional media you have selected. Often you will receive immediate feedback from which you can informally judge learning effectiveness and student reaction. You may even make some adjustments on the spot. However, the next step will fully indicate your success or failure.

Step Six—Administer the Posttest

Give the criterion-referenced posttest to determine the extent to which students have achieved your objectives.

Step Seven—Analyze and Interpret Test Data

After giving the criterion-referenced pretest and posttest, you are in a position to make decisions about your instructional system. The pre- and posttests can be compared using descriptive statistics. Mean gain can be noted and a related t test used to ascertain statistical significance. However, individual gain scores are most important for accountability. Check each student's terminal performance level. Has every student attained the objectives? Have all students achieved your predetermined minimum criterion score?

If your test is valid and students have achieved your objectives, you have been successful. However, if students have not learned you must analyze the reasons for instructional failure. Here are some possible problems and solutions based upon the accountability model:

1. Students did not understand or accept objectives. Clarify objectives or revise them if they are ambiguous or irrelevant. Tell the student what is expected of him—what he is expected to be able to do. Secure commitment to objectives, perhaps by contract.
2. Students did not possess prerequisite behaviors. Modify

pretest to measure needed prerequisite competencies. Review prerequisites. Stimulate student recall of previously learned concepts and skills. Provide remedial instruction where needed.

3. Instructional strategies were inappropriate or ineffective. Model expected behavior. Provide for the following: demonstrations; active participation of each student; interaction with media, teacher, and other students; enough practice time; appropriate drill material; feedback; self-evaluation; individual differences in learning rates and learning styles.

4. Media were not effective or not utilized. Get help from a media specialist. Take a workshop in instructional technology. Read references (see Appendix B).

5. Criterion test was not valid. Rework the test items for a representative and valid sample. Develop a more appropriate form or type of test.

6. Only a few students failed the criterion level. Recycle those students through the instructional tasks until they reach criterion level.

Step Eight—Modify the Instructional System on the Basis of Analysis

Test analysis and interpretation will provide a plan to modify the system for necessary improvement. The system is a quality control process with improvement built in by design. The feedback loop of Figure 7-1 illustrates that each component of the system can be modified in recycling. If adjustments cannot be made, the instructional system may be dropped from the program. An alternative system could then be developed.

Using the Eight-Step Approach

To help clarify the preceding discussion, an actual account illustrating the use of the eight-step approach is presented here. It began with a teaching problem related to a class in conducting. Students were having trouble analyzing music because they had limited knowledge of musical form. I decided that programed material could be developed to serve a remedial function without taking up limited class time.

Step One. The mini-course was laid out in behavior/content modules leading to terminal performances. Several possible behaviors were considered in the initial list of objectives. The learner could define, identify, diagram and construct (compose) the formal elements and formal types. "Identify" was judged to be the most critical verb. The student must identify the formal components in order to analyze. The other behaviors were utilized for interim objectives. Some of the actual course structure is discussed in Chapter 3 and illustrated in Figure 3-2.

Step Two. After objectives were delineated, the criterion test was constructed. It consisted primarily of specific musical examples to be analyzed by identifying formal elements, cadences, design and formal types. There were 160 points possible in the final version. Students were required to achieve an 85 percent exit score.

An entry test was developed to determine if students could classify chords by name, function, inversion and Roman numeral. It was assumed that music majors could read music, although one sometimes wonders. Cadence names, types and effects (functions) were included in the pretest.

Step Three: Since the strategy called for individualized study units the major instructional medium was programed material. I wrote the basic text, keyed it to appropriate musical examples, and had an I.T. specialist program it.

All musical examples were recorded on audio tape. Transparencies were made of diagrams of the basic formal types. I developed supplementary projects consisting of specifications for composing period structure and small forms.

Step Four. The pretest was administered. Only one student achieved criterion level.

Step Five. Programs and supplementary materials were given to all students. The audio tapes and visuals were available for individual use. A time of three weeks was suggested as reasonable to complete all projects. Students could work at their own pace, however, and elect supplementary studies as desired.

Step Six. The posttest (exit test) was administered.

Step Seven. The data were analyzed. The mean (average) gain score was 76.9. This was statistically significant. However, nineteen of the thirty-six students failed to reach the criterion score. Students were recycled through the program and supplementary material until they attained the minimum test score.

Step Eight. Analysis of data revealed mistakes, weaknesses, and ambiguities in both the criterion test and program. Item analysis of the test identified unclear and invalid test questions and examples. One puzzling discrepancy was the inability of students to diagram forms (an interim behavior), even though they could analyze the examples. It would seem that the interim behavior was unnecessary and confusing as it was presented in the program.

The programed learning transferred to the classroom when similar music was used. The method of analysis helped students rehearse and interpret music for performance, e.g., move phrases to cadence. The program has been used in subsequent classes, with modifications and with better provision for different learning styles. Some students find the linear program format tedious and boring. Textbooks, compositional approaches, and tutoring are alternatives available to students.

Performance Contracting

One important tactic of accountability is the performance contract. A performance contract (contract of accountability) is an agreement entered into by a school system with a teacher, a group of teachers or an outside agency. The contractor agrees to produce specified results within a designated period of time for a certain fee. Since both parties contract for specified changes in student behavior, objectives must be agreed upon at the outset. The contractor may use whatever procedures and media he chooses, subject to preliminary review and approval by the school representative. The method of evaluation is also determined in advance. It will provide the evidence or "proof of results." Thus a performance contract is not only an agreement for services to be rendered (like the usual teacher contract), but also for outcomes to be achieved. This latter stipulation is the unique aspect of the performance contract. The contractor is paid in proportion to the accomplishments of his students as measured by the assessment instruments. An outside auditor is usually secured to independently verify the results.

Educational Engineering

Leon Lessinger proposes seven steps that lead to a system-wide adaptation of innovative educational programs through performance contracting.[1] The procedure allows for the development and trial of a new program before it is permanently installed into the curriculum, providing minimum risk for existing programs, teachers and administrators. The steps are briefly outlined below.

1. The official representative group of the school system— the "local educational authority" (LEA)—obtains money for development of the proposed program. It can be budgeted locally or acquired from a federal, state or private funding agency.
2. The LEA selects a "management support group" (MSG) consisting of people with the expertise and experience to serve as long-term consultants.
3. Next, the MSG, in cooperation with the LEA, school staff, community and others, produces the "request for proposal" (RFP). This is a set of specifications for the educational results to be achieved.
4. The RFP is now sent out for bids. Private firms and non-profit agencies that respond are invited to the "pre-bidding conference" (PBC).
5. Based upon this conference, a final RFP is written and released, and formal bids are secured. The LEA, aided by the MSG, selects the most promising bids and invites the bidders to present their proposals in further detail, using

---

[1] See Leon M. Lessinger, *Every Kid A Winner: Accountability in Education* (Palo Alto, California: Science Research Associates, 1970), pp. 36-7. Read the entire book for a complete report on accountability and performance contracting.

demonstrations, exhibits and sample teaching materials. Specific questions are answered at this time.

6. The LEA, with the assistance of the MSG, evaluates the proposals and selects what it considers to be the best total package. Negotiations for the performance contract then begin.

7. At this time the LEA hires an "independent educational accomplishment auditor" (IEAA) to monitor the implementation of the performance contract and to assess the results upon which payment will be based.

Writing the Performance Contract

There is no universally agreed-upon format for a performance contract. Understandably, a contract is developed in a unique situation for purposes specific to that situation. However, several items are commonly included.[2]

A performance contract usually opens with an introductory statement of goals and purposes to connect the proposal (RFP) to the specifics of the contract. This section can include broad descriptions of benefits, methods, costs and modes of proof that demonstrate contractor accountability. In general, these statements provide an overview to clarify the intent of the contract for professional and lay people. The following list illustrates the types of specific items that can be included in the subsequent sections.

1. Objectives that specify in detail the learning to be accomplished by each student
2. Student target population
3. Student entering characteristics
4. Total length of the program (a semester or a year)

---

[2] See Frank W. Johnson, "Performance Contracting With Existing Staff," *Educational Technology* XI, No. 1 (January, 1971), p. 61, and Albert V. Mayrhofer, "Negotiating a Performance Contract," in *Educational Accountability Through Evaluation*, E. Wayne Roberson, ed. (Englewood Cliffs, N.J.: Educational Technology Publications, 1971), pp. 75-91.

5. Schedule of meeting times
6. Procedures to be used
7. Media to be used
8. Grouping of students
9. Facilities needed
10. Support personnel
11. Management specifications
12. Clerical needs, supplies, forms
13. Costs
14. Constraints of time, personnel, costs, equipment, etc.
15. Criteria of acceptable performance
16. Tests to be used
17. Educational audit requirement

Contracting for Music Programs and Classes

Performance contracting has been most frequently used to help students who have not acquired basic skills in reading and mathematics. However, current trends tend to support a more extensive utilization of this technique. Perhaps the whole idea may seem somewhat tenuous for school music programs. For example, Lessinger has warned that contracts used casually may accomplish nothing, and when used "wrongly" can cause harm, especially when the desired results are not easily measurable.[3] Yet music teaching has a long history of private enterprise, best exemplified by the competent studio teacher at one extreme and the now-you-see-him, now-you-don't "music man" on the other. Although many of us have "moonlighted" with dance jobs and private teaching, the position taken here is not advocating bonuses and incentives for music teachers, but adequate *support* for music programs.

Why should an administrator allocate resources for developing a new music program or class when money is short and time is precious? Why should he continue to support an existing program? Obviously administrators have allocated much money for music. But music is facing hard times. The performance contract offers one

---

[3] Lessinger, *Every Kid A Winner*, p. 68.

approach to hard-headed administrators and board members for needed money and support, especially when objectives are derived from the goals and philosophy of the total school system. Essentially you say, "I will do this (in terms of stated behavioral objectives), given the time, facilities, equipment, personnel, and money. I guarantee my students will learn—each one of them!"

Most opposition to performance contracting is directed toward the modes of testing and the dangers of commercialism. Refer back to Chapter 6 where the first concern is investigated. Problems arise when norm-referenced measures are used as indicators of performance and teachers "teach for the test." More comprehensive criterion-referenced tests must be developed. The second concern can be dealt with by teachers on an "in-house" basis. They can compete with private firms by using the systems model, the procedure of performance contracting.

Managing the System

The accountability approach, with its emphasis upon individualized instruction, requires an overwhelming amount of bookkeeping. In addition to the knowledge explosion, there is a corresponding proliferation of essential data in the systems approach regarding each student's attainment level, learning rate and learning style. This practical management problem must be solved before any actual program can be put into operation. Many teachers give up the systems idea at this point. They have students by the hundreds, seas of nameless faces, a different class every twenty minutes, or large performing organizations with very little rehearsal time and too many performances. How can records be kept for all these students to monitor their progress toward objectives? The amount of information to be collected seems to have passed beyond human control to the point where electronic data processing is needed. Since the computer is not readily available to most teachers, alternative methods are suggested here to cope with this aspect of systems management.

Folders should be compiled for each student and records kept of his progress toward the stated objectives. A chart listing students'

STUDENT PROGRESS CHART

Class _____

Student's name	Steady beat	Melody beat	Steady & melody	Echo clapping	Reading rhythms	Writing rhythms	Hearing intervals	Reading intervals	Singing in tune	Instruments

Procedure:

Steady beat: Played record—clapped even pulse.

Melody beat: Clapped rhythm of the words.

Steady & melody: Steady beat in feet and rhythm of the words in hands

Echo: beat 8 beats of ti's and ta's on bongo.

Reading rhythms: 8 measures of ti's and ta's half's and whole's—clapped.

Writing rhythms: Played on woodblock 4 beats of ti's and ta's or 8 beats of half's and whole's. Students wrote rhythm patterns.

Hearing intervals: Played on recorder, smsm, slsm, mrd, smd, drm. Student wrote patterns.

Reading intervals: Notes on staff and symbols. Sung with names. 1. smslsmd, 2. mslsd, 3. drmsls

Singing in tune: Gave pitch, played harmony on recorder.

Instruments: Students played sm, sls, mrd, dms on Orff instruments.

Figure 7-3

names and the objectives is helpful. Objectives can be identified by number or otherwise coded on the chart. Figures 7-3, 7-4, and 7-5 are actual forms that have been used in public schools. In Figure 7-3 objectives are described briefly in each column and specified by procedure in the right margin. The teacher could never remember the current status of each child without such charts.

Students can help keep class records to free the teacher for more important teaching duties. Paraprofessionals provide another possible source of help. There is yet a third way to solve the problem. Some teachers use wall charts to serve both record-keeping and decorative functions. As each objective is mastered, the student colors in the appropriate square any way that he wishes. This adds interest and individuality to the charting procedure while again freeing the teacher to teach. Each student can see his own progress. He becomes further interested and excited about musical activities. Charts help to direct learning and guide teaching.

Mention was made in Chapter 6 that the grading system must be adapted to the type of objective being assessed and the concept of mastery learning. Thus a "grade" may often consist of a simple pass or no-pass designation. Figure 7-6 is a musical grade card utilizing a three-point scale—Good (G), Fair (F), or Not Yet (NY). The "not yet" classification is fitting for the systems approach. Students who have not achieved criterion level are recycled through alternate methods and media until they can achieve the objectives.

Self-Check Mastery Test

1. What are the four phases and eight steps of the systems approach to instructional development described in this chapter?
2. Select an objective for your class and outline the systems approach to its achievement.
3. Select objectives and write a performance contract leading to their attainment in your teaching situation.
4. How can you manage the copious data that accrues from systematic instruction?

ELEMENTARY WIND INSTRUMENTS
PROGRESS CHART

STUDENT'S NAME	Inst. Care					Tone				Rhythm							Symbology						Ensemble					Instrument Played
	1	2	3	4	5	1	2	3	4	1	2	3	4	5	6	7	1	2	3	4	5	6	1	2	3	4	5	
1.																												
2.																												
3.																												
4.																												
5.																												
6.																												
7.																												
8.																												
9.																												
10.																												
11.																												
12.																												
13.																												
14.																												

Class _____
School _____
Teacher _____

Figure 7-4

JUNIOR HIGH SCHOOL STRINGED INSTRUMENTS
PROGRESS CHART

STUDENT'S NAME	Left Hand Technique								Inton.			Right Hand Technique					Rhythm—Bowing								Ensemble							Performance			
	1	2	3	4	5	6	7	8	1	2	3	4	1	2	3	4	5	6	7	8	1	2	3	4	5	6	7	8	1	2	3	4	5	6	7	1	2	3	4

Figure 7-5

MUSIC REPORT CARD
5th GRADE

_____
Name

G = Good

F = Fair

NY = Not Yet

1. Can sing in tune.   _____

2. Can sing a harmony part.   _____

3. Can sing a phrase of music using combinations
   of Do, Re, Mi, So and La.   _____

4. Can clap combinations of whole, dotted half, half,
   dotted quarter, quarter, eighth and sixteenth
   notes.   _____

5. Can compose a four measure rhythm using whole,
   dotted half, half, dotted quarter, quarter,
   eighth and sixteenth notes.   _____

6. Can accompany the class on the auto harp playing
   a 3 or 4 chord song.   _____

7. Can accompany the class on the Orff Melody Bells
   using an ostinato (repeated pattern) which is original.   _____

8. Can clap a series of whole, dotted half, half, quarter,
   eighth and sixteenth notes while the teacher taps
   the beat.   _____

9. Can create a composition in ABA, AB or Rondo Form
   in a group situation.   _____

10. Can play a phrase or song on an Orff instrument.   _____

11. Does actively participate in Music Class.   _____

Dear Parent,
You may wish to keep this report and note your child's
progress in Music by comparing it with future reports.

Figure 7-6

appendix a

the accountability approach
in today's schools

This section consists of several examples of the accountability approach as developed and used by music teachers in the field. Space will not permit the inclusion of all collected materials, or even a complete statement of the selected curriculum content. The resulting excerpts, however, should help you relate the approach to your music teaching.

The quoted selections are not finished products of ideal programs. They are examples of various ways that music teachers have put the systems approach to work to improve instruction and move toward an accountable program.

Using Individual Student Learning Packets to Reach Objectives

Douglass Campbell, Bloomfield Hills Schools, Michigan

Terminal Performance Objective (Listening, Music 1.00)

Given recorded examples of music, at his level of instruction, the learner will describe the music in terms of any two of the following:

1. The usage or design of elements
2. Form and/or function
3. Performance media
4. Period or style that the music represents
5. Texture
6. Content (programmatic implications)

An Enabling Objective (Music 1.15, Intermediate level)

Upon hearing a musical example the (fourth-sixth grade) student will describe the music in terms of the predominant element(s) with at least 75% accuracy. The musical elements include melody, harmony, rhythm, tempo, dynamics and timbre.

Assessment (Pretest and Posttest)

STUDENT INSTRUCTIONS	ANSWER SHEET
After hearing each excerpt, write the name of the most important element, i.e., the element that has been changed, altered or emphasized more than the others.	64._____
Melody Tempo	65._____
Harmony Dynamics	66._____
Rhythm Timbre	67._____

Teaching Strategy

[*Student Packet, consisting of worksheets, audio-taped narration and musical examples, is excerpted below.*]

THE ELEMENTS OF MUSIC
PART II

A. *Gregorian Chant*:

   (1) Circle the name of the element that appears to be lacking in this music.

RHYTHM   MELODY   HARMONY   TEMPO
              DYNAMICS   TIMBRE

(2) Circle the name of the element that seems to be the
      most important.

RHYTHM   MELODY   HARMONY   TEMPO
              DYNAMICS   TIMBRE

B. *Questions to ask yourself while listening to music*:

MELODY:

Is there one melody? Is the melody repeated? When the
melody is repeated, is it changed at all? Does the melody
seem to be the important part of this composition?

RHYTHM:

Does the rhythmic feeling change within the composition?
Is the rhythm the central part of this composition?

HARMONY:

Does the harmonic feeling change within the composition?
Does the feeling of harmony seem to be the important part
of this composition?

TEMPO:

Does the speed of the composition change? (faster or slower)

DYNAMICS:

Does the volume or loudness or softness change within this
composition? Does it change quickly or gradually?

TIMBRE:

Is part of the interest created by a change of instruments or
voices?

DIRECTIONS TO THE FOLLOWING QUESTIONS:

You will hear 5 examples of music. Each example illustrates
the change of at least one element within the composition,
for the sake of interest. Draw a circle around the word which
describes that change.

1. *Hospoldi Pomilui*   MELODY   TIMBRE   HARMONY
2. *Hava Nageela*   DYNAMICS TEMPO   HARMONY
3. *Surprise Symphony*   DYNAMICS MELODY   TEMPO
4. *Blue Bells of Scotland* TIMBRE   MELODY   HARMONY
5. *Pines of the Appian Way* TEMPO   HARMONY   DYNAMICS

Using the System to Teach Ternary Form

Norma R. Farmilo, Walled Lake Consolidated Schools, Michigan
[*See Worksheet, Figure 7-2*]

Objective
Given an example of ABA form, the fourth-grade student will identify the form as being ABA, with 80% accuracy.

Assessment (Pretest and Posttest)
Instructions to the teacher: Sing ten examples of songs in simple forms (AB, AA, ABA and ABC) in which each part consists of a short two to four measure phrase, e.g., *Twinkle, Twinkle Little Star*. Have the student circle YES on the answer sheet if the song is ABA, or NO if it is not ABA. The student must answer eight correctly to pass.
Instructions to the student: You will hear ten songs. Some of them will be in ABA form. Circle YES if the example is in ABA form. Circle NO if it is in some other form.

Entering Behavior
The student can identify a phrase. He can identify like and unlike phrases.

Teaching Strategies
　　　1.　Have the class sing two familiar songs as *Frere Jacques* and *Make New Friends* to "construct" an ABA form, i.e., *Frere Jacques* (A), *Make New Friends* (B), *Frere Jacques* (A). Stress that the first part is the same as the last part. The middle part is different.

2. Have students create other compositions in ABA form using familiar songs.

3. Use rhythm instruments to create the B part, i.e., song (A), percussion (B), repeat song (A).

4. Create a rain storm with body sounds or rhythm instruments in ABA form, e.g., rain (A), thunder and lightning (B), rain (A).

5. Send small groups to an adjoining room with rhythm instruments to "compose" an ABA form. Have them perform for the rest of the class who evaluate the composition and ABA structure.

5. Have students listen to examples of ABA form. Use recordings and live performances by teacher and students. Bring in non-examples for comparison.

7. Use balloons or large cards marked with "A" and "B." Have students hold them up at appropriate times.

8. Use overhead transparencies to illustrate different sections of songs. Use different colors for A and B. Draw diagrams on transparencies to clarify form. Also use pieces of glass in similar shapes and colors to depict "A" and "B". Set them on the stage of the projector.

9. Use commercially available multi-media packages that present ABA form, as *Music 300*.

Recycle students through the various strategies if they do not meet criterion level on the posttest.

Media

Use record player, records, overhead projector, transparencies, projectors, filmstrips, slides, series books, etc. as needed.

Some Third Grade Music Objectives with Report Card and Record Form

Janet E. Shultz, Oak Park Schools, Michigan

1. Given a beat the student can clap whole, dotted half, half, quarter or eighth notes. Teacher taps beat and says,

"whole note." Student claps whole notes until teacher asks for a different note, etc. If student makes no mistakes, teacher records G (good). If student makes up to three mistakes, teacher records F (fair). If more than three mistakes are made, teacher records NY (not yet).

2. Given a beat the student can clap a rhythm using a combination of whole, dotted half, half, quarter or eighth notes. Rhythm written on board. Four measures long. In 2/4 or 4/4. Student has three chances. No mistakes=G. One mistake=F. Two or more mistakes=NY.

3. The student can give the beat of music played by the teacher. Teacher plays at least four phrases of music in 2/4, 3/4 or 4/4. Student claps beat with accent. Student identifies beat for rating.

4. The student can correctly place note heads for Do, Mi, So and La on the staff. Teacher has staff on board. Teacher tells student where So is. Student places note heads on staff for following combinations (either one or two). Do-Mi-So-La, So-La-So-Mi, etc. No mistakes for G. One mistake for F. Two or more mistakes NY.

5. The student can correctly sing combinations of Do, Mi, So and La. Example of exercise on board. S M S M, S L S M, S M D D, D M S S, etc. Student will sing four sets like the example with hand signals. Teacher gives student starting note. Student has three chances. No mistakes G. Two mistakes F. Three or more mistakes NY.

6. The student can clap the rhythm of a familiar song while someone else claps the beat. One attempt. Four phrase song. While class is singing or alone. One or two mistakes G. Three=F. More mistakes=NY.

7. The student can clap the beat of a familiar song while someone claps the rhythm. No mistakes for G.

8. The student can sing in tune. Four phrase song.

9. The student can sing a simple round with the teacher.

10. The student actively participates in music.

G—Good

F—Fair   Music Report Card

NY—Not Yet   3rd Grade

Name

1. Given a beat can clap either

2. Given a beat can clap a rhythm written on the board using combinations of

3. Can give the beat of music played by the teacher.

4. Can correctly place note heads on the staff for combinations of Do, Mi, So and La.

5. Can correctly sing a melody using combinations of Do, Mi, So and La.

6. Can clap the rhythm of a familiar song while someone claps the beat.

7. Can clap the beat of a familiar song while someone claps the rhythm.

8. Can sing in tune.

9. Can sing a round with the teacher.

10. Actively participates in Music.

Record of Student Progress

	clap notes	clap rhythms	identify beat	place notes	sing patterns	clap rhythm of melody	clap beat	sing in tune	sing round	participates
Music, 3rd	1	2	3	4	5	6	7	8	9	10
Jeff		G			G				NY	
Don		F								NY
Jean		NY			G				G	

[*The preceding is an example of how a record of each child's progress is kept. A regular record book is used with a list of all children
in the class on one page.*]

Using Formative Evaluation in Junior High Boys Choir

Larry Wolf, Oak Park Schools, Michigan

HOW AM I DOING IN BOYS' CHOIR?

NAME_____

RHYTHM SKILLS

____1. I can clap back a simple 8-beat rhythm pattern
while keeping the beat with my feet.

____2. I can play at least two distinct rhythm patterns on
the bongos (from those learned in class) while
matching the beat with a recorded piece of Sergio
Mendes. I must be able to play each pattern at
least four times in a row correctly in this manner.

____3. I can perform he following sequence of rhythms,
twice each, without any errors, matching my beat
with the Mendes record.
            1...5...
            12..56..
            1.34.67.
            1......8
            1.345.78
            1.3...7.

SINGING SKILLS

____1. I can sing *500 Miles* (verse or chorus) by myself
in a key that fits my range, staying in tune throughout. No piano help.

_____2. I can sing "do" while another sings "mi" keeping for at least 3-5 seconds. No piano help.

_____3. I can sing my part to *Sloop John B.* (or *Noble Duke of York*) by myself, while another sings the other part. I stay in tune and sing the notes correctly.
_____"with a little help" from the piano
_____without any help from the piano

_____4. I can sing my own part to the song *Viva Tutti* (pp. 2-5) correctly and in tune—
_____with two others singing the other parts and the piano helping
_____with two other boys singing the other parts— no piano.

READING SKILLS

_____1. I can identify by letter name all the notes of the treble staff, plus notes up to two leger lines above and below.

_____2. I can identify by letter name all the notes of the bass staff, plus notes up to two leger lines above and below.

_____3. I can read correctly (clapping or "tah-ing") any rhythmic pattern in 4/4 time using eighth, quarter, half, dotted half and whole notes (rhythm sheet #1).

_____4. I can correctly perform from notation, rhythmic patterns using dotted quarter and eighths, syncopation, sixteenth notes, and various rests (rhythm sheet #2).

_____5. Given a piece of music and told where the tonic note ("1" or "do") is located, I can correctly give the number names of any other pitches in the music.

_____6. I can locate "1" or "do" of any flat key in major mode by examining the key signature.

_____7. I can do the same with any sharp key in major mode.

_____8. I can determine the pitch number of the first note in a song (major mode), from the key signature.

_____9. Given a selection from FSS in a major mode and

the pitch for "do" I can determine the key tone and sing pitches and rhythm accurately (Intervals: 2nds, 3rds—rhythms: same as #3 above. Errors allowed: 3. Length: at least 32 beats).

____10.   I can locate and follow my own part in open or closed score (2, 3, and 4-part music).

        ____I can locate and follow any other part too.

Study Contract for Survey of Music Class

Gordon Sabin, Coldwater Schools, Michigan

I, the undersigned student of Coldwater High School, agree that I will accomplish the following during the marking period ending_____.

I further agree that my own work will be evaluated by myself and the instructor according to the criteria set forth below and that the grade received for this work will be my nine week marking period grade. I affirm that I have assisted in the development of the work project and in deciding upon the type of evaluation to be employed in my case.

_____
signature of student

PROJECT:

I plan to work in the area of_____.

Specifically, I will accomplish the following task(s):

_____
_____
_____
_____

The evaluation will be based upon the following observable behavior(s):

_____
_____
_____
_____

Upon completion of this project my grade will be_____.

_____
signature of instructor

[*Author's comments*: *The Survey of Music class at Coldwater High School is a general music class offered for full credit to any student regardless of musical background. There is no curriculum in the traditional sense, since students elect various areas of study based on their interest and aptitude. The instructor's role is one of a resource person and keeper of records. Students are free to achieve or not achieve as their aspirations, talent, and ambition dictate.*

Each student's work unit is stated in behavioral terms in a contract. The contract specifies the learning objectives, method of evaluation, grade, and amount of time for completion agreed upon by both instructor and student. Students may confer with the instructor during the marking period to alter their contract. However, no changes are allowed after the eighth week. In this way students are encouraged to keep close track of their own progress and make a realistic appraisal of their own achievement. Students not completing their contract at evaluation time receive a failing grade for that marking period regardless of the contracted grade.

The class is based on a concept of independent study. The student may seek help from any source at any time but no help is forced on him or even suggested to him without his solicitation. The class meets in a large square room with six small practice rooms located along two sides. There is a stereo record player with earphones and a variety of records. Assorted musical instruments including pianos, guitars, percussion and wind instruments, and a library of reference books in theory, history, biography and instrument instruction are available in the room for student use.]

Using Objectives in a Marching Band Guide

Carl Stone, Detroit Schools, Michigan

[*To the student*]

Now that summer vacation is over it is time to put ourselves back into gear and get ready for the coming season . . .

The following is a set of objectives that we use throughout the marching season as guidelines for achievement. Let us all work together to accomplish these objectives . . .

MARCHING TECHNIQUE

To maintain a position in the band, each bandsman must demonstrate the following:

Within first week of rehearsal

1. From verbal command by director, drum major or rank leader, the bandsman will perform all facing movements (Right and Left Face, Attention, and Parade Rest) using appropriate oral sounds for each movement with an accuracy of 90%.

Within second week of rehearsal

2. Upon hearing a command whistle from director or drum major, the bandsman will respond to the whistle appropriately using correct oral sounds (if any) with an accuracy of 90%.

Within third week of rehearsal

3. Given a formation chart, the bandsman will locate himself on the football field as indicated on the chart with an accuracy of 100%.

4. Given a "patterns in motion" chart, the bandsman will follow the prescribed directions as indicated on the chart with an accuracy of 80%.

5. Starting on the goal line of a football field, the bandsman will march 100 yards using eight steps to every five yards at M.M. 120 with an accuracy of 90%.

6. Starting on any prescribed yardline of a football field, the bandsman will march fifty yards using eight steps to every five yards while playing movement music at M.M. 130 with an accuracy of 90%.

7. Starting on any prescribed yard line of a football field, the bandsman will march backwards both while playing and not playing using eight steps to every five yards covering a distance of at least ten yards with an accuracy of 100%.

8. Provided a drum cadence, the bandsman will march at least ten yards using eight steps to every five yards at M.M. 240 with 99% accuracy.

9. Provided a drum cadence, the bandsman will march at least forty yards using eight steps to every five yards at M.M. 20 with an accuracy of 90%.

10. Provided a drum cadence, the bandsman will move both arms in appropriate directions with less than 10% deviation.

Other requirements

11. From memory, the bandsman will march through the "block band dance" within one week from start of project with an accuracy of 80%.

12. From memory, the bandsman will march through and play appropriate music for that dance within two weeks from start of project with an accuracy of 90%.

13. From memory, each bandsman will perform with the entire band the upcoming band show within a period of two rehearsal sessions before the performance with an accuracy of 95%.

MUSICIANSHIP

1. Given written music, the bandsman will play the music at its prescribed tempi two days after receiving it with an accuracy of 90%.

2. From memory, the bandsman will perform all music that requires movement of the body (excluding "block band dance" music) at prescribed tempi, a minimum of two days before a scheduled performance with 100% accuracy.

3. With the use of written music, the bandsman will perform all music that is to be played in a stationary position a minimum of two days before a scheduled performance with 100% accuracy.

4. From memory, the bandsman will perform the school song, school fight song, spirit boosters and pep songs at all football games and pep rallies, at the command of the director, with 99% accuracy.

5. From memory, all drummers will play the "Death" Cadence and cadence Number One by end of the first full week of rehearsal with 90% accuracy.

ATTENDANCE REQUIREMENTS

To maintain a position in the band, each bandsman must do the following:

1. Given proper notice, each bandsman will attend extra

rehearsals with no more than one unexcused absence.

2. Following regular band rehearsals, each bandsman will attend all marching practices with no unexcused absences.

3. Daily, each bandsman will be ready to rehearse five minutes after the tardy bell for that period with no more than three unexcused tardies.

4. Whenever the band has a performance, each bandsman will be there at the time set by the director, in full regalia, ready to play. The director will only excuse bandsman prior to performances after weighing the validity of the request.

APPEARANCE

1. Before each performance, the bandsman will present for director, drum major, or rank leader his properly dressed uniform. It must meet the satisfaction of the person judging.

2. Before each performance, the bandsman will show the director, drum major, or rank leader a polished and operative instrument. It must meet the satisfaction of person judging.

Using Objectives in a Guide for Senior High School Concert Band

Richard T. Saunders, formerly Livonia Schools, Michigan

To the student

The following pages contain an outline or schedule that is designed to direct and encourage your continued musical growth . . .

The standards set forth in the schedule are maximum rather than minimum standards. That is to say that these are the requirements for achieving an "A" each semester. We encourage you to make them *your* standards for achievement. [*The introductory material continues to describe five proficiency levels, from "Musician I" to "Master Musician V" and their relation to grading.*]

Testing for the various levels will be scheduled periodically. Announcements will be posted prior to test days. A list of all instrumental students and their respective "Levels" will also be posted after each test period . . . [*Levels I and IV are included below for illustration.*]

MUSICIAN — LEVEL I

To acquire the Level I rating, the student must demonstrate the following degree of performance proficiency and musical knowledge:

1. Given notation, the performer will be able to play seven major scales, of his own selection, each in two octaves, with correct fingerings, using eighth notes, at M.M. 120, with 90% accuracy.

2. Given notation, the performer will be able to play a two-octave chromatic scale, in eighth notes, using correct fingerings and four different styles of articulation of his own selection, at M.M. 100, with 90% accuracy.

3. Given notation, the performer will play rhythmic examples in 2/4, 2/2 and 6/8 meter, selected from "127 Original Exercises for Band," by Grover Yaus, at M.M. 100, with 90% accuracy.

4. Upon request, the performer will play a prepared solo, of his own selection, demonstrating his current level of musicianship and technical competence.

5. Without the aid of the instruction sheet or other materials, the performer will demonstrate a minimum knowledge of the care and maintenance of his instrument by scoring 80% or better on an oral examination.

MUSICIAN — LEVEL IV

To acquire the Level IV rating, a student must demonstrate the following degree of performance proficiency and musical knowledge:

1. Upon request, the performer will sustain a concert B$^\flat$, for sixteen counts, at M.M. 72, beginning at pianissimo and continuing to a crescendo to a fortissimo at the sixteenth count, with no more than 5 cents deviation from true pitch as indicated on a Conn Strobotuner.

2. Given notation, the performer will be able to play all fifteen major scales, each in two octaves, with correct fingerings, using sixteenth notes, at M.M.104, with 90% accuracy.

3. From memory, the performer will be able to play a chromatic scale, in two octaves, using correct fingerings, using eight different styles of articulation, in sixteenth notes, at M.M. 104, with 95% accuracy.

4. Given notation, the performer will play rhythmic examples in 2/4, 2/2, 6/8 and 3/8 meter selected from "127 Original Exercises for Band," at M.M. 126, with 95% accuracy.

5. Upon request, the performer will present an intonation plotting chart indicating the relative pitch deviation of each chromatic note on his instrument, throughout his entire playing range, once he has tuned that instrument to a concert F on the Conn Strobotuner.

6. Upon request, the performer will play a prepared solo, of his own selection, demonstrating his current level of musicianship and technical competence.

7. Upon request, the performer will present the director with a research paper covering the history and development of his own instrument, including the names of three current outstanding professional performers of virtuoso stature and a list of their recordings if available. This paper should be of sufficient length to cover the subject thoroughly (not less than 750 words), footnoted, and should contain a bibliography.

[Author's comments: I feel very strongly that this type of a program might stimulate some thinking among both directors and their students regarding purposes and "accountability." In other words—where are we going—where have we been?

At the end of the year I had an informal discussion with several of the students who participated in the program. The most frequent response from them was that by setting a series of short-term goals I had encouraged them toward a project of self-improvement that they would otherwise not have undertaken. They all agreed that we should continue with the program. The highest level attained during the first year was Level IV.

As you might have guessed, organizing and maintaining a pro-

gram such as this consumes a tremendous amount of time. All of the examinations were given after the regular school day. I found that I had to allot at least twenty minutes for each proficiency examination. The majority of the students found it necessary to come in twice to complete the requirements. We kept a list of names posted indicating which students had achieved which levels of performance. Grades and seating within the Music Ensemble were determined primarily by achievement relative to the proficiency examinations.]

A Junior High Wind Instrument Curriculum Consisting of 47 Tasks Keyed to Specific Method Books and Reference Materials

Ran Evans, Oak Park Schools, Michigan

3. *Task*: Perform #4 on Page 6, FDBM (First Division Band Method) III

   Given: Instrument and music

   Restrictions: No assistance

   Time allowed for completion: No time limit

   Number of possible attempts at completion 2

   Minimum speed: (♩ =86 Part 1), (♩ =86 Part 2)

   Evaluation reference: according to adherence to rhythmic, phrasing, dynamic and tonal notation of printed music

   Number of errors allowed: 2

   Date of completion_____

   Teacher's signature_____

4. *Task*: Identify 25 half-step and whole-step intervals by writing a "W" under whole steps or a "H" under half steps.

   Given: Series of 25 printed half-step and whole-step intervals

   Restrictions: No use of printed aids; no assistance

   Time allowed for completion: 15 minutes

   Minimum speed: Not applicable

   Evaluation reference: Accuracy of answers according to music theory information sheet.

   Number of errors allowed: 5

Date of completion_____
Teacher's signature_____

5. *Task*: Write seven one-octave ascending major scales in
     whole notes
   Given: A list of 7 keynotes on Page 28 of the FDBM
   III, manuscript paper
   Restrictions: No printed aids; no assistance
   Time allowed for completion: 20 minutes
   Evaluation reference: according to the printed notes of
   these same scales found in the unit on major scales
   found on Page 28 of the FDBM III.
   Number of errors allowed: 3
                          Date of completion_____
                Teacher's signature. _____

6. *Task*: Perform two octaves of the chromatic scale, as-
     cending and descending
   Given: Instrument
   Restrictions: No assistance or printed aids
   Time allowed for completion: No time limit
   Number of possible attempts at completion: 2
   Evaluation reference: Initial note to be that of the chro-
   matic scale exercise on Page 20 of FDBM III; finger-
   ing accuracy according to instrument fingering charts,
   Page 2, FDBM III
   Minimum speed: ♩ = 120
   Number of errors allowed: None
                          Date of completion_____
                Teacher's signature_____

8. *Task*: Perform seven major scales one octave ascending
     and descending
   Given: list of key names of 7 major scales appearing on
   Page 28 of FDBM III and instrument
   Restrictions: No printed music or assistance: no repeat
   of top tone
   Time allowed for completion: Not more than 10 seconds
   allowed between each scale performance
   Number of possible attempts at completion: 1
   Minimum speed: ♪ = 120
   Evaluation reference: Accuracy according to consistent

tempo as well as correct notes as listed in FDBM III.
Number of errors allowed: one incorrect scale

Date of completion_____

Teacher's signature_____

30. *Task*: Write definitions of 13 musical dynamic markings

Given: List of 13 dynamic markings found on page 33, FDBM III

Restrictions: No printed aids; answers must be written verbal statements

Time allowed for completion: 10 minutes

Number of possible attempts at completion: 1

Minimum speed: Not applicable

Evaluation reference: accuracy according to congruity to definitions of these terms on page 33, FDBM III

Number of errors allowed: 2

Date of completion_____

Teacher's signature_____

40. *Task*: Write a 1 or 2 next to given number on an answer sheet to indicate the best of two tape recorded examples with respect to tone quality

Given: Ten pairs of tape-recorded, single-line, eight-measure melodies performed on various wind instruments; numbered answer sheet

Restrictions: No printed aids

Time allowed for completion: Each pair of examples will be played only once with a pause of five seconds between each example of the pair and a pause of ten seconds between each pair.

Number of possible attempts at completion: 1

Minimum speed: None

Evaluation reference: Subjective evaluation

Number of errors allowed: 2

Date of completion_____

Teacher's signature_____

41. *Task*: Perform Etude 1, 2, 3 or 4 on page 27, FDBM III

Given: Instrument and instructor-selected exercise music

Restrictions: No aids
Time allowed for completion: No time limit
Number of possible attempts at completion: 2
Minimum speed: ♩ = 76
Evaluation reference: according to adherence to rhythmic, phrasing, dynamic and tonal notation of printed music
Number of errors allowed: 2

Date of completion_____

Teacher's signature_____

45. *Task*: Perform Watkins-Farnum *Performance Scale A*
Given: Instrument and *Performance Scale A*
Restrictions: No previous practice
Time allowed for completion: According to test directions
Number of possible attempts at completion: 1
Minimum speed: According to listed tempos
Evaluation reference: accuracy according to adherence to rhythmic, phrasing, dynamic and tonal notation of printed music
Number of errors allowed: Final score of no less than 55 of 100

Date of completion_____

Teacher's signature_____

Objectives for High School Music Appreciation

Frank Irish, Rochester Schools, Michigan

A. Historical information

1. Given a list of characteristics of musical style, the student will identify those characteristics which are descriptive of Renaissance, Baroque, Classical, Romantic, Impressionistic, and Contemporary periods in music with 70% accuracy.

2. Given a list of composers, the student will identify the composers as Renaissance, Baroque, Classical,

Romantic, Impressionistic, or Contemporary with 70% accuracy.

3. Given unfamiliar examples of non-musical arts (painting, literature, architecture, sculpture) the student will relate them to relative time periods of music history with 30% accuracy.

B. Musical elements

1. The student will identify duple, triple, and compound meters on hearing recorded examples three times each with 70% accuracy.

2. The student will identify examples of polyphonic, homophonic, and fugal style on hearing recorded examples three times with 50% accuracy.

3. The student will identify the instruments of the orchestra and voice classifications of singers by sound on hearing recorded examples once with 70% accuracy.

4. The student will identify the instruments of the orchestra by sight with 90% accuracy.

5. The student will identify examples of music in major and minor modes in recorded compositions on two hearings with 70% accuracy.

6. Given the form of a specific composition, the student will identify the place in the form where the music stops with 60% accuracy on two hearings. The stopping points to be identified will be exposition, development, or recapitulation in sonata-allegro form; principal song, trio, or repeat of principal song in song and trio form; and statement of theme or number of the variation in theme and variations form.

C.   Musical terminology

Given a list of musical terms, the student will identify
their definitions with 70% accuracy.

D.   Listening awareness
1.   The student will identify the period of style of an
unfamiliar composition with 50% accuracy.
2.   Given the list of Palestrina, Bach, Mozart, Beethoven, Tchaikovsky, Debussy, and Stockhausen or a
similar list of composers identified strongly with
styles of music, the student will be able to identify
unfamiliar compositions as being their works with
50% accuracy.
3.   The student will listen actively with observable attentiveness to an unfamiliar composition without
the incentive of reward or punishment.
4.   The student will verbalize his response to an unfamiliar composition in essay form to the teacher's
satisfaction after three hearings.

Sample Test Items for Objective B6

Listen carefully to each example. Indicate where we are in
the form when the music stops.
1. _____
Main theme First Var. Second Var. Third Var. Fourth Var.
2. _____
Principal song   Trio   Return of Principal song
3. _____
Exposition   Development   Recapitulation

Guitar Instruction in the High School

Roy E. Ernst, formerly Livonia Schools, Michigan

Learning the guitar provides students with the capacity for independent music making. Satisfying results can be obtained without
maintaining a demanding practice schedule.

The guitar lends itself to teaching practical music theory. Because the guitar is a fretted instrument, it provides both an audio and a visual perception of music.

OBJECTIVES OF GUITAR I:

1. The student will be able to tune his guitar with the aid of a tuning fork.
2. Students will be able to accompany songs using tonic, subdominant and dominant chords in the major keys of C, G, D, and in the minor keys, of a, e, and d.
3. The student will develop fluency in the use of at least six strumming patterns.
4. The student will be able to play accompaniments for at least twelve songs of his own choice.
5. Students will be able to read melody, rhythm, meter signatures, chord symbols and tablature at a level of difficulty found in typical folk songs.
6. Students will be encouraged (but not required) to compose and perform original songs.

Behavioral Objectives and Criterion-Referenced Test Items for a High School Music Theory Course

Beverly J. Labuta, Roeper City and Country School, Michigan

The goal of the high school music theory course is to develop the functional musicianship of each student. The following objectives were derived from this goal . . . Objectives leading to skills of traditional part writing were excluded because they could not be validated with reference to the goal . . . Students composed music extensively to augment the prescribed objectives.

. . . To make any course "accountable" there must be some way to assess the attainment of objectives. Therefore, each objective includes a sample test item.

3. OBJECTIVE: Upon hearing a rhythm pattern, the student will notate the pattern with no more than two errors.

TEST ITEM: Listen to the rhythm pattern, which is in 4/4 meter, and notate it on your paper.

5. OBJECTIVE: Given a starting note, the student will construct one octave major scales inserting accidentals with no more than two errors.

TEST ITEM: Write a one octave major scale above each of the given pitches.

8. OBJECTIVE: Given a written root note, the student will insert a second note to form the indicated interval with no errors.

TEST ITEM: Write the interval asked for above each root note.

M3   P4   m3   m7   m2   P5   M6   M7

10. OBJECTIVE: Upon hearing intervals played on the piano, the student will identify them with no more than one error.

TEST ITEM: What is the interval you hear? (Teacher plays the following intervals: M3, P4, m6, M7, m2, A4.)

11. OBJECTIVE: Given a root note, the student will construct major and minor triads with no errors.

TEST ITEM: Construct a major or minor triad as indicated above each root note.

M m m M m M m M

12. OBJECTIVE: The student will play major and minor triads with 90% accuracy.

TEST ITEM: Play the following triads on the piano:

A♭M   GM   am   dm   EM

e♭m   F♯M   c♯m   DM   fm

13. OBJECTIVE: Upon hearing major and minor triads the student will identify them as major or minor with no errors.

TEST ITEM: The teacher will play major and minor triads on the piano. Indicate upon your answer sheet if the triads are (M) major or (m) minor.

18. OBJECTIVE: Given a simple chord progression consisting of primary chords (I, IV, V), the student will harmonically analyze the progression with no more than one error.

TEST ITEM: Analyze the following primary chord progression.

19. OBJECTIVE: Upon hearing a simple chord progression consisting of primary chords, the student will harmonically analyze the progression with no more than one error.

TEST ITEM: Listen to this chord progression consisting of primary chords and write the correct symbol for each chord. It will be played twice.

22. OBJECTIVE: Given a written example the student will classify cadences as Half, Plagal, Deceptive, Perfect Authentic or Imperfect Authentic with no errors.

TEST ITEM: Write the type of cadence beneath the given examples.

24. OBJECTIVE: Given a diatonic melody, the student will compose an accompanying harmonic progression to the satisfaction of the teacher.

TEST ITEM: Write a harmonic progression for the following melody.

26. OBJECTIVE: Given a root note, the student will construct a major-minor 7th chord with no errors.

TEST ITEM: Construct a major-minor 7th chord above each given root note.

28.   OBJECTIVE: Upon hearing Dominant 7th chords in a progression the student will identify the 7th chords with no errors.

TEST ITEM: The teacher will play a chord progression on the piano. Harmonically analyze each chord, marking the Dominant 7th chords you hear.

Using a Unipac to Teach Beginning Strings

Shirley Kehr, formerly Detroit Schools, Michigan
[*Instructions to students*]

Name_____   Date_____

When you have completed this UNIPAC, you will be able to look at most music and know how to play the correct note. To do this, you will be learning these things:

A.   How to let the alphabet help you figure out names of notes.
B.   How to let the alphabet help you figure out which finger to place on which string.
C.   How to tell whether the music is for your instrument.

When you have finished the unit these are the specific things you will be able to do:

A.   Identify your clef sign, state its name, and name the line which takes its name from your clef.
B.   Name any note within the staff and those outside of the staff which can be played by your instrument.

C. Write, state, and demonstrate how any of the above notes may be played on your instrument.

You will not be expected to memorize all of these notes immediately. You will be expected to figure out how to name and play any note and to do this you will need to memorize four notes now.

[*This is followed by a Pretest and four lessons. Lesson Two is presented here.*]

Lesson 2

Title: Naming the rest of the staff
Objective: When you finish this lesson, you will be able to name a note on any line or space of the staff.

These are notes:

As you can see, there is something about each note that is the same and something else which makes each note different. There is one thing that all notes have. Can you say what it is?

First of all, they don't all have stems, do they? Which one does not have a stem? Some are filled in and some are not. How many are filled in? Some have extra lines attached to their stems. But the one thing they all have in common is the fact that they have a round shape. In this lesson, it is the round shape which is most important. No matter what kind of a note you see in this lesson, always look for the round shape. (It is called the head and that makes sense, doesn't it?) Wherever the head is placed on the staff is what **is** important.

Now see if you have that idea in mind. Below are some notes on a staff. Under each note is a blank to fill in. You are to write which space the note is in. (Remember to count from the bottom.)

Your answers should have been these: in the first blank is 1. In the second blank, 3. The third blank is 2; and the last note is in the 4th space.

Below are some line notes. (The ones you just did were space notes.) Line notes have a line running through the middle of them. When people say a note is "on the line" they are talking about line notes. Which lines are these notes on?

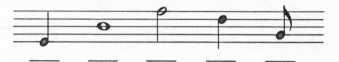

You should have answered in this order: 1, 3, 5, 4, 2.

Now see if you can tell the line notes from the space notes and still name the correct line or space. If a note is on the line, mark it L and put the number of the line beside the L. If it is a space note, mark S and the number of the space.

Are you ready to check your answers? Make sure you have a letter and a number on every blank.

L 1   S 2   S 1   S 4   L 4   L 2   L 3   L 5   S 3

If you made any mistakes, go back and check your work to see if you understand what you did wrong. If you got them all right go ahead.

The rest of the job is simple because the only other thing you need to know is the alphabet. In fact, you only need to know the first seven letters of the alphabet. Take a few minutes to say them over a couple of times. The important thing is to be able to say the letters fast and start over without slowing down. You should be saying a b c d e f g a b c d e f g a b c . . . etc. Now if you find that too easy try this. Say them backward. That will take some practice, but don't forget—if you can learn to say them one way, you can just as easily learn to say them another way—like backwards. Try it again: g f e d c b a g f e . . . etc.

What you need to do now is remember where the line is that has the same name as your clef sign. When you place a note on that line it also has the same name.

    G   C   F

When you place notes on the other lines and spaces you just say the alphabet.

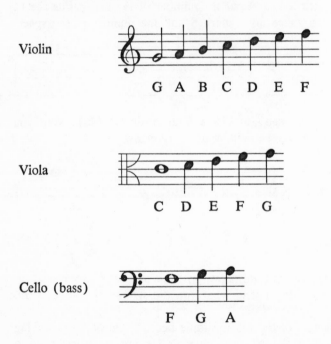

Violin

      G A B C D E F

Viola

      C D E F G

Cello (bass)

      F G A

What about the other lines and spaces, especially for the cellos and basses? As you see above, when the notes go *higher* in the staff, you say the alphabet forward. Can you guess what happens when you go *lower* in the staff?

Violin

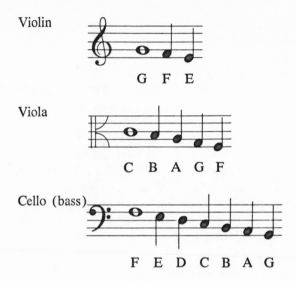

G   F   E

Viola

C   B   A   G   F

Cello (bass)

F   E   D   C   B   A   G

If you said *backward*, you were correct. When notes climb *higher*, the alphabet goes *forward*; when notes slide *down* the staff, the alphabet goes *backward*.

There is just one more important point to make and that is this. You can only use the alphabet when the notes climb by going line-space-line-space . . . etc. If the notes skip a line, you must skip a letter. If the notes skip a space, must you also skip a letter? The answer to that question is "yes." What if the note jumps further? How many letters would you skip if the notes jumped over a line *and* a space? The answer is two. What if the notes jump over two lines and one space? See if you can name these notes.

The answers are:

Violins: G B C E

Violas: C E G F

Cellos (bass): F A G E

If you got every note right, go on to the exit test for this lesson. If you missed any notes, read the part below which is written for your instrument.

Violins: The first note is the line note which gets its name from your clef. So this note is *G*. The second note skipped over the space (*A*). The note after A is *B*. This should have been your second answer. The third note follows as close to B as it can get. Its name is *C*. The fourth note again skips over a space and so there is no D. Your last answer should have been *E*. Now try this example to see if you understand.

The answers are G F# A B E. If you missed any, you should go back to the beginning of this lesson. If you got these right, go on to the exit test now.

Violas: The first note is *C*. It is on the line which is named after your clef sign. From there, the next note skips up to the next line. This means the space D was skipped over and the second note is *E*. The same thing happens with the next note. The space F is skipped and the third note is *G*. From there the note goes back down to the *F* that was just skipped over. Now try this example to see if you understand.

The answers are C, B, D, F, E. If you missed any, you should go back to the beginning of this lesson. If you got them all right, go on to the exit test now.

Cellos (basses):   The first note is *F*. It is on the line that is named after your clef. From there the next note skips up the next line. This means the space G was skipped over and the second note is *A*. From there, the note goes back down to the G that was just skipped over. After that, the next note skips over F and jumps down to *E*. Now try this example to see if you understand.

The answers are F, E, D, F, A. If you missed any, you should go back to the beginning of this lesson. If you got them all right, go on to the exit test now.

EXIT TEST FOR LESSON 2

Name the notes in your staff.

Answers to Exit Test

Violins:
E A G E D B F C F

Violas:
F B A F E C G D G

Cellos (basses)
G C B G F D A E A

If you got every answer correct, go to lesson 3. If you missed one or two, try to figure out what your mistake was. If you know what went wrong, go on to lesson three. If not or if you missed more than two, go back to the beginning of this lesson. If you still have trouble after studying the lesson again, see the teacher before you go any further. Do not try to go ahead if you don't understand this lesson, because the next lesson depends upon your being able to name any note in the staff. The next lesson will show you the name notes outside of the staff.

[*Author's comments: A UNIPAC is a packet of self-instructional materials designed to teach a single concept or idea. It includes behavioral objectives, pre- and posttests, and self-evaluative devices. Lesson Two of the four lessons in this UNIPAC is included here.*

The lesson begins with a simultaneous presentation of the stimuli (the different types of notes). The common link is elicited by the question at the end of the paragraph. (What do the notes have in common?) The next paragraph is designed to suspend the answer a while longer and to do this, the discussion names items which are not common to each member of the class. Finally the answer is given.

The important learning here is not so much the concept of "note" as it is the principle: "head of the note is most important." But the concept "note" must be present first. To test acquisition of the principle, three sets of notes are presented. The student has already learned to count lines and spaces from the bottom in the previous lesson. This is recalled so that other elements will not interfere with the lesson.

Answers must be immediately confirmed so they are located near the questions. If students merely copy answers into the blanks, they will not be able to pass the posttest after completing the unit.

Another principle is introduced (the alphabetic relationship to naming notes on a staff) and practice is provided. The relevant clues are suggested in preparation for the final problem in this lesson—naming notes that skip lines and spaces.

Throughout the lesson there are opportunities for confirming responses, practice in using the newly acquired principles, and finally a real problem—to figure out any note within the staff. Problems are solved by using principles. The three primary principles involved were introduced one at a time in the lesson.]

appendix b

selected source guides
for instructional media

Educational Media Index
Fourteen Volumes, 1964
McGraw-Hill Book Company
New York, New York
Music and Art are included in Vol. 3.

EPM—Educators Purchasing Master
"Instructional Materials," Third Edition, 1971
Fisher Publishing
3 West Princeton Avenue
Englewood, Colo. 80110
Music teaching materials are topically indexed, pp. 164A-169A.
Elementary music materials are listed, pp. 219-222.

Film Guide for Music Educators
  by Donald J. Shetler
  MENC-NEA
  1201 Sixteenth Street, N.W.
  Washington, D.C. 20036
  1968

Index to 16 mm Educational Films
  Second Edition, 1969
  National Information Center for Instructional Media
  University of Southern California
  Los Angeles, California 90007
  Printed by:
  R.R. Bowker Company
  1180 Avenue of the Americas
  New York, N.Y. 10036
  Films are cross-indexed by subject matter, title and annotated
    listing.
  Other indexes available from the same source:
  Index to Overhead Transparencies, 1969
  Index to 8mm Motion Cartridges, 1969
  Index to 35mm Educational Filmstrips, 1969

Learning Directory
  Seven Volumes, 1970-71
  Westinghouse Learning Corporation
  100 Park Avenue
  New York, N.Y. 10017
  Music listings are found in "Instructional Materials Index," Vol.
    5, pp. 4102-4138. Each listing is categorized by grade level,
    A-V medium, title, size, date, and source. The most compre-
    hensive listing available is to be revised and reissued annually.

Music and Phonorecords
  The National Union Catalog (Library of Congress)
  Three Volumes, 1963-67
  Edwards Publishers, Inc.
  Ann Arbor, Mich. 48104
  1969

Technology In Music Teaching
  Music Educators Journal
  Vol. 57, No. 5, January, 1971
  See especially p. 97 ff

Words, Sounds and Pictures About Music
  The University of the State of New York/The State Education
    Department, Bureau of Elementary Curriculum Development
  Albany, N.Y. 12224
  A multimedia resource listing for teachers of music, grades K-6

index